WILL THE REAL MR. BUTT(UP

(A LOVE STORY)

Once in a lifetime, you may meet a giant among men; someone who has the charisma so powerful that you feel you can reach out and touch it. What is charisma? It is the ability to inspire and it is at its most powerful when it is founded on serenity.

We had just returned home from a conference at the Guild Hall in London. Alan had peed on the carpet there. So that had put rather a damper on the event. We had already had entered via the kitchens. This was the only accessible way in for a wheelchair user. Disability discrimination? This was 45 years ago.

I am talking about Alan my husband. He was injured in 1969 aged 29, at work. He was helping to move a printing machine and it toppled over onto him breaking his neck. Still don't know why he got involved in helping. He was not even a printer, but a technical illustrator. Wrong place, wrong time.

I remember, saying to him earlier that week "please don't go in to work to help with the move,

Saturday." I so enjoyed our weekends together and I was so pleased to be able to spend time with him. Love eh?

The year is 1969.

We had just bought a house, Alan, myself and our 4-year-old son. We moved in June 1969. What a challenging year that was! And also indeed the years that were to follow. The house needed updating. Alan was very good at DIY and had started to re-vamp the kitchen. He had taken out the door at the end of the kitchen and knocked a hole through the side of the house. It was semi-detached. Where the original door was Alan had blocked that up and put a window in, with sink underneath, with a view over the lovely, long garden that backed onto allotments. The hole in the side, was hung temporarily with an old curtain. We didn't seem, in those days, to have to worry about burglaries.

July 1969, I was busily painting the inside of the new kitchen cupboard. They were just basic wood with no finish. The next day into hospital, where our 2nd child, a daughter, was born on July 11th, then July 21st Man landed on moon. "One giant step for man", there were to be lots of "giant steps" for us to follow. When the health visitor paid us a visit a few days later, there was a look of horror on her face to see the 'bomb site' state of the kitchen. The year went on. Alan was doing free-lance illustrating in the evenings to get money together to pay for materials to pay for updating the house. I remember him saying "oh I wish I could go away from here and come back to find it all done" - be careful what you wish for, that is exactly what did happen! It was October and Gavin's 4th Birthday. We spent it round at Nans for a Birthday tea. The house was still in no fit state for entertaining. NOVEMBER.....

THE INJURY

It was 13th November 1969, the firm phoned me at home, to say Alan had injured his shoulder and they would send a car to collect me and take me to the hospital.

Strange the injured shoulder. 40 years later my daughter was thrown from a horse and again, the hospital thought it was a damaged shoulder. But it transpired that she had ruptured an artery in her neck which had induced a stroke. But I digress.

I quickly bundled my 2 children up to my neighbour. Gavin was 4 and Lorna just 4 months old. On arriving at the Central Middlesex hospital Park

Royal, the doctor informed me that Alan had suffered a spinal injury at level C5 and was paralysed from the neck down. They would be transferring him the next day to The National Spinal Injuries Unit at Stoke Mandeville Hospital in Buckinghamshire. I had never heard of the hospital - it was soon to become a focal point in our lives.

I had to return home with this alarming news to my 2 children being cared for by my uncomplaining neighbour and the rest of the family, Alan's mum and dad and my sister and brother-in-law. I still remember standing in the kitchen and vowing I would take care of Alan.

The first visit to the hospital the following morning, I tried to lean over him to give him a kiss. But was abruptly told not to do that. I suppose his condition was so fragile this gesture might have made things worse.

We were waiting for the ambulance to take us to Stoke Mandeville. Alan had even overnight developed a pressure sore on his heel. There was quite a delay because the lift had broken. So instead of waiting any longer a party of porters and nurses 'bumped' Alan down the flight of stairs to the waiting ambulance. This was with a patient with a serious spinal injury - horrors!! Then we had the

40mile journey travelling along the A40 on a Friday evening with a police escort and going at a snail's pace to avoid any bumps in the road. You can imagine the tail back of frustrated workers trying to get home that Friday evening for the weekend. There was no air ambulance in those days.

We arrived late in the evening at the ward, in darkness, to be met by the sister. She told us this would be Alan's home for the next 9 months. They allowed me to stay that night. The following morning, I had to say goodbye to him, neither of us knowing what lay ahead of us. "Please visit Jan, I desperately need you" said Alan.

I returned home, to rescue my kids from my dear neighbour Joyce. She turned out to be my anchor during all of the following years. Time after time, I would go 2 doors up to cry on her shoulder, in despondency. Never ever did she turn me away, even though, she perhaps had other things to do.

And so, the next few months was a new routine. I visited Alan every afternoon and onto into evening. A total of an 80-mile round trip. My mother had moved in to help with the children.

It became increasingly difficult to find 'taxi' volunteers to take me to Stoke Mandeville. So, I had to take up driving again. I had never enjoyed driving and tried to avoid it if possible. There were some scary moments. I especially remember driving home in thick fog, I was so relieved to see the lights of the Target pub on the A40 - nearly home. Phew!

When I visited Alan for the first time, at the spinal unit, he was lying flat on his back. He had skull callipers attached to his head holding it in traction. This was to stabilise the injury. They had a type of periscope fitted to the bed, whereby the patients could see what was happening around them in the ward. A few days later Dr. Hancock took me into a side room. He explained that my husband was severely disabled and paralysed in all four limbs. This was as a result of his injury. This was a crush fracture at level C5. (C4 is the level that people would be hung at.)

See Appendix re spinal cord information.

Spinal cord injury is an age-old problem, but it wasn't until the 1940s that the prognosis for long-term survival was very optimistic. Prior to World War II, people routinely died of infections to the urinary tract, lungs, or skin. SCI went from a death sentence to a manageable condition. Nowadays, people with spinal cord injury approach the full life span of nondisabled individuals.

To explain more, the level at which injury occurs affects different areas of the body, so at C5 deltoid shoulder muscle is affected, C6 wrist, C7 Triceps, C7-8 fingers, T1 hand, T2-T12 Trunk, T7-L1 abdomen, T11-L2 ejaculation, L2 hips, L3 quadriceps, L4-L5 hamstrings -knee, L4-S1 foot, S2 penile erection, S2-S3 bowel and bladder.

So, the level injury Alan sustained meant all these were affected. There is also the involvement of the autonomic nervous system. You can understand that Alan was pretty well 'broken'. Plus, no amount of "determination" will overcome a damaged spinal cord!! I could not believe that the doctor was talking about my Alan. On one occasion when I turned up at the ward, he had a massive trolley type thing by his bed. Good Lord I thought, now what? These were the days when it was usual to see people in 'iron lungs' as a result of the disease polio. Sigh of relief, it turned out to be the meal trolley!! Our first Christmas that year was spent visiting Alan. I took the children, dressed in their best clothes. Usually, I had left them at home. I will always remember a big black doctor taking Lorna and dancing around the ward with her in his arms. She was now 5months old.

The 6 weeks passed with Alan in bed and then he was allowed up into a wheelchair. I must admit I walked straight passed him on that next visit. Just did not recognise him in a wheelchair. Another thing that would annoy him if anyone was pushing him in a wheelchair, they would leave him parked the wrong way. Facing a wall for example. Just not thinking. Anyone able bodied would turn to face the way THEY wanted. The next few months were spent down at the gym, with his physios, Gail and Leonora. They worked on him tirelessly during his rehab. They were trying to restore any movement to his limbs. It was here that I learnt the 'standing cervical transfer lift.' This entailed, whilst Alan was sat in the wheelchair, me grabbing hold of his waistband on his trousers, and then starting a rocking movement and on Alan's count of 3 leaning back and letting Alan push himself upright. Stepping back if necessary, to make sure his weight was over the balls of his feet, and then, with his feet on a swivel plate turn to be lowered into the wheelchair. This was to prove invaluable in my ability to manage him physically. Also, great importance was instilled on dressing and positioning, to do everything possible to avoid any pressure sores. This was because all sensation of discomfort was now gone. Toes on socks pulled forward, shoes laces not tied too tight, undergarments waistband etc not wrinkled. Just anywhere that might cause pressure. It was drummed into the patients if you got a pressure sore it was "your fault" (Alan use to ask us to pull him over sideways in his chair to, as he said "ease his bum"). He had no triceps to enable him to raise himself from the seat.

Pressure ulcers (also known as pressure sores or bedsores) are injuries to the skin and underlying tissue, primarily caused by prolonged pressure on the skin.

Back to Stoke Mandeville (ward 2x)

Sister Mears frightened the life out of me and I am not the sort to be easily intimidated, despite my diminutive 4'7" stature!! But If I tried to sneak into the ward before the 2pm visiting time, I would get severely reprimanded and told to go back outside and wait. But my goodness that ward was run to such an extremely high standard. There were 12 beds on the ward. Some with higher level of SCI than others. Not much sympathy was metered out by the orderlies. I remember Alan relating the tale of one newly injured chap. This patient was calling out "Ow, Ow, it hurts!" to which the orderly replied "Course it bloody hurts, you've broken you f… neck!" Perhaps this was the way to deal with the patients! A case of man up!!

There were moments of light hearted banter. The song of the moment was Cliff Richard singing "Congratulations", this was translated to the patients singing, at the top of their voices "evacuations" - more of this later.

Another time, a visit from the occupational therapist to the chap in the next bed to Alan. She had the task of showing him how to do basket weaving. The patient was a good, typical, East End publican. He had a low spinal injury, so had full use of his hands. He said to her "You know exactly where you can shove your basket weaving!". "Oh, come now, was the reply, you are in no position to talk like that." Quite a few chuckles went around the ward!

But there were the downsides. One of the young patient's wife was pregnant and she decided she could not face this sort of life and left him. Such a nice chap, too. He later came down to visit us in Devon. His father had been killed in the same RTA which had left Ray paralysed. So, his dear elderly mum had to take on Ray's care as a widow. So brave!

In the first days I would cling to any news of other people who had been spinal cord injured and glean any information about the eventual outcome. What sort of recovery rate was there? This was such a massive learning curve. I really think people assume that a tragedy as this couldn't possibly happen to them YES IT COULD AND DOES. When I see lads tomb stoning, I cringe with what might be the outcome. Even recently saw someone dive into a lake. OH, that is a major incident of a 'broken neck' People around me seem to do such different dangerous things, that could possibly end up with their lives shattered.

Later on, I was to visit another SCI person and his wife to give them some counselling. It became apparent that the wife was already becoming impatient with his needs. I went home to tell Alan that I didn't think the relationship would last. Later we heard that he had committed suicide. Never did understand how he got the top of the bottle of pills.........Here was some who's hands were completely paralysed?

HOME

Eventually Alan was allowed home for weekends. I had to learn how to cope with this man who was entirely reliant on me for all his physical and emotional needs. One of the most import things I had to learn about was a condition called Autonomic Dysreflexia. This could lead to hypertension and death if not treated. People with a spinal cord injury above T6 were predisposed to this life-threatening condition and it could be considered a medical emergency. The main symptoms were clammy hands, profuse sweating and generally feeling unwell. The main triggers were a full bladder and or full rectum. This I had to rectify. A medication called nifedipine was always ready to hand. We never left the house without them.

Another condition was low blood sugar levels. Alan would feel 'woozy'. For this we always had glucose tablets available.

Due to the level of injury, Alan had lost the ability to control bowel and bladder function, leaving him doubly incontinent. Consequently, I had to perform a manual bowel evacuation, with him lying on his side in the bed, which could take up to an hour. The lower bowel had to be completely emptied. So, hopefully avoiding any later accidents. Then after thoroughly washing the whole area, it was necessary to glue a condom onto his penis to facilitate urine drainage into a "kipper". A rubber container for the urine. This had to washed out thoroughly and disinfected. But still used to smell foul.

Horror, I had no idea what to do, but Alan talked me through these procedures. Mum was keeping the kids out of the way downstairs. We had not had any communications from the local district nurse, but he was sent home with all the required equipment i.e., suppositories, disposable gloves, waterproof sheets, condoms, rubber tubing and the kipper, from Stoke Mandeville. Alan was eventually discharged from Stoke Mandeville in early Autumn 1970. Nine months after his accident. Mother had left to return to help with Aunt and Uncles guest house. And so, his life of struggling to survive began.

WELCOME HOME

We had been married for just 6years.

That 1st Christmas at home in December 1970, Alan spent downstairs in a bed in the dining room, watching his 2 children opening their Christmas presents. There was an enormous amount of presents from so many people who had heard of Alan's accident and had felt so sorry for his children. He had been sleeping downstairs, using an' ikey' (old Derbyshire saying, for rubbish) commode on hire from the Red Cross. The house was still with bedrooms upstairs. It was rather difficult doing bed evacuations etc. with young children and their friends running about. The local authorities had suggested that we move into a special development for disabled people, but Alan was adamant that his children would not grow up surrounded by people in wheelchairs.

There were lots of things to remember when caring for Alan. The injury left him with a loss of sensation, i.e., he couldn't feel hot, cold or pain below upper chest level. Also, he was very spastic - which meant his legs would go into spasm, perhaps kicking anyone within reach. Although latterly his daughter Lorna would balance on his spasming leg pretending to be riding a horse – maybe that's where the equine love affair for her started??!! The only way to break this spasm was to bend his big toe back. Or by putting pressure on his knee.

Over the years these things became second nature to me. He could manage to hold a cup if you placed it with his finger through the handle and make sure it was not too hot to touch. He did at one time get a nasty burn on his shoulder from having a wheat bag put there which was too hot. He could only breathe via his diaphragm, so any hint of a chest infection was serious, not having the ability to cough etc. Also, his body's temperature control had been knocked out, similar to a new born baby. His body would not react if he became too cold, so he always had to keep warm. But conversely, in the summer he could not be allowed to get over heated, always with a hat on and covering on his neck. He used to later revel in sitting in our summer house in the garden in Devon, which was under some trees, so therefore never got too hot. But Alan was out in the fresh air.

A Normal Day.

This was the routine:

MORNING ROUTINE

7am. Get up. Get Alan onto commode. Very ancient one on loan from the Red Cross.

7.30 start preparation for bowel evacuation.

7.40 get children up and start on their breakfast.

7.50 digital clearance of back passage and swabbing rectum. Glue urine drainage condom onto penis and attach to drainage bag. This used to be called a 'kipper', made of rubber and would smell horrible, even after sterilisation.

Transfer back to bed.

8.00 check children re breakfast.

8.15 nurse arrives to wash and dress patient. It would always be a bone of contention that district nurses would not perform a manual bowel evacuation. Even on trips to a general hospital they were unwilling to perform this task. This was to become a serious issue later in life during stays in hospital when the nurses would refuse to carry out a manual bowel evacuation.

I get Gavin ready for school.

8.40 neighbour collects Gavin to take him to school

Months later, I remember taking Lorna down to school, and having to rush back to do the MBE for Alan, before the nurse was due in. (the nurses would NOT perform this operation).

Nurse leaves. Get Lorna dressed. Prepare packed lunch for Alan.

Finish dressing Alan for journey to work. Hair combed; watch put on.

Put coat on Lorna, and strap into child seat in car. Get Alan into car.

Leave for work

10.30 arrive at work. Get Alan into wheelchair. Get Lorna out of car and take with Alan into the office. The lady there would always give Lorna some jelly tots.

Return home. I remember the 1st morning after taking him to work. I got home and the doorbell rang. It was the district nurse. I told her she was too late I had already got Gavin to school and taken Alan to work.

Well, my dear. she said, you must get yourself well organised the night before' Oh, I thought, how many mornings have you got a quadriplegic husband up and ready for work and, 2 children also got ready? This was to be my first encounter with district nurses. Some were angels' others could have me in tears. For instance: -

One nurse threw the full urine drainage bag onto the floor of the kitchen and it exploded all over the floor. She could not be bothered to go upstairs to the toilet to empty it. Well, she said, "we leave that for the relatives to empty!". This with young children running in and out! Another time someone else forgot to pop a hole in the urine drainage condom, which would not allow the urine to drain into the bag, so therefore urine-soaked trousers on a trip, another trip out spoilt, having to return home. Afterwards I stuck a post-it note saying please remember to pop the condom. I was told indignantly "we are not children"! Maybe not but do your job properly!!

Then whilst Alan was having a spasm one time, to be told by a nurse "don't be frightened", not understanding spasms! Sigh….. And one asking what tetraplegia was. All adding to Alan's frustrations.

EVENING

Dinner eaten all together. I had to always cut up Alan's food and place the cutlery strap onto his hand, then slip a fork into it.

Evening spent as a family with the children.

Get children to bed and then the longer task of getting Alan to bed.

Clothes taken off. Upper clothes first and pyjama top put on. Alan had no core strength, so I had to support him whilst putting on the top. Then lay him across the bed to take of shoes and socks. Then dragged up the bed and take of trousers, by rolling from side to side. Pillows between knees and under feet. This was to preventive any pressure. Feet stood upright, and not with any likely hood of rubbing together. Empty drainage bag and connect fresh one. This to be emptied at night if needs be. There were nights and (sometimes during the day,) when despite all precautions Alan's incontinence would become obvious. And the onerous task of stripping bedding and disposing of faeces and wet bedding, could take up most of the night.

We eventually persuaded the local authority to let Alan have a ripple mattress. This had pockets of air that inflated and deflated, thereby avoiding any pressure sores. (Bye the bye, one night whilst changing Lorna's nappy I accidently stuck the nappy pin into the mattress – oops! Deflated!) Large glass of squash with straw. The straw was necessary because the glass could not be held to his lips whilst lying down. This was to help flush kidneys through during the night. I had to hold the glass whilst he drank.

Example of a DAY TRIP TO LIBRARY.

Arms into sleeves of coat, overhead adjust.

Crutches on, cervical lift stand,

 adjust trousers, urine bag, testicles, into wheelchair.

Open car door, park wheelchair alongside, cervical lift, swivel into passenger seat.

Keys into ignition, pull out choke. Seat belt on. Shut door.

Chair into boot.

Arrive.

Chair out of boot, cushion on chair, footplates up.

Lift from car, swivel into chair

Remove keys, shut door.

Push up ramp into library.

Reach down selection of book from shelves, place on table for perusal.

Push back to car. Reverse procedure to get back into car. Keys in ignition, shut door, chair into boot.

Home

Wheelchair out of boot. open door, swing legs out. Lift into wheelchair.

I would drive car into garage into house take of coat, hang up. Give library books. Make coffee/tea.

TYPICAL EXAMPLE OF THINGS UNABLE TO DO

Can you image one of the many things someone has to carry out for Alan was to blow his nose for him. I got to know just how hard to squeeze the nostrils and what sequence.

Things I had to attend to for Alan: Peel orange, fold letter, place into envelope and stamp. eat boiled egg in egg cup, peel banana, undo beer can, drink in bed, unless straw placed in cup/glass. read in bed, use scissors, open doors, unless fitted with long hand, not knob. open windows. answer door. Switch on lights, fire, TV. undo screw top bottles. take car into service, or car wash. get into or out of car unaided. Undo boot. open car doors, cut finger or toe nails, shampoo hair, tie shoe laces, clean shoes. Do up buttons. THE LIST WAS ENDLESS.

Alan used to get so cross when people would say to him "What you want to do…"

Mornings, before nurse arrives, I had to do the MBE as the nurses would NOT undertake manual bowel evacuation.

Also, we only had a nurse to help on two mornings a week. No evening, weekend or bank holidays visits.

Return from taking children to school. Ring on toilet. insert suppositories, lift from bed onto chair, into toilet, from chair onto toilet. Carry out manual removal. remove drainage bag. Swab rectum seat on chair with urine bottle. wait for nurse to arrive. This could be almost immediately or an hour later.

Seat in dining room, I had already given toast and coffee whilst waiting for nurse. Get cigarettes and matches. (I know he did eventually give up) give post, undone. Called in to take telephone messages. Massage neck. This was to be a troublesome ache, always. Cook lunch, lunch together. Cut up Alan's food, and give fork in holder. serve coffee, give tablets. Stand up transfer to settee. Turn on TV. Fetch book, turn on fire. light cigarette. Empty drainage bag. massage bottom. Get tissues for nose. Help to blow. Children home from school. Usual family time with children, sometime their friends here, or round to their house. Evening meal, then another cigarette. And so, the day ends.

NIGHT TIME

Several times during.

Turn and adjust drainage bag Check for pressure marks. Empty bag if necessary. Sometimes a bowel movement in bed. The cleaning and changing could take up most of the night.

On one of the occasions, we took a neighbour's children to see the Royal Tournament, Gavin had a dreadful coughing fit. We realised it was all the dust thrown up by the Kings Troop Horse Brigade performance, that triggered the asthma. Which was another burden, poor lad, that he had to endure along with a disabled father. We did try very hard, to give them a normal childhood as possible. But the physical side of their relationship with their father could never be attained. They both did respect him.

Alan had been a very active man before his accident. Motorcycling, which included racing at Brands Hatch, rugby, playing scrum half for Old Actonian's, swimming, motoring, including car maintenance, art and reading. Being a practical man, home maintenance came easy. We had just brought our first house in June 1969 and he was in the process of modernising it when he had his accident. So, for some time we had to live in a 'bomb site'! When the health visitor came to check on Lorna, born that July, she was, to say the least, shocked about how we were living. Actually, I can remember Alan saying "I just wish I could leave one morning and when I got back the place would be finished" - Be careful what you wish for, as that was exactly what happened. Fortunately, there was a very good builder living just a few doors down, who said he would finish making the kitchen habitable.

In February 1972 the firm offered him a return to work, albeit as a menial office clerk and a reduction in salary. Before his accident he was employed as a technical illustrator. Drawing exploded views of machine tools - similar to those in Haynes Car manuals. This meant me driving him to work every day. (see morning routine.)

Return to work.

This was really a non-starter. He couldn't reach the filing cabinets. People had to fetch and carry for him all day long. And the need for someone to empty his urine drainage bag was not a task that anyone volunteered for. At one stage he was offered a training course for disabled locally. But on arrival Alan was faced by a flight of stairs! Errmmmmm…… Who thought of that idea…….?

In March 1971 he was offered a book-keeping course at Queen Elizabeth's Training College for the Disabled at Leatherhead. He was to 'give it a go'. He really didn't think it would work, as if his hands were so paralysed that he could not continue his career as a technical illustrator, how would he be able to fill in ledgers by hand? This was in the days before everyone used computers and accountancy software. The welfare officer of the college was to say "whilst there is no doubt whatsoever of his ability to carry out the work of book keeping, there are the practical limitations imposed by the assistance he needs due to his paralysis". Also, another task was finding volunteers to drive him down to Surrey on Sunday evening, after his weekend home. I had the two children in bed. More difficulties. I used to count the week off before he would be finished at the 'funny farm' as we called it. I missed his company so much. A joy to have him home on Friday evening, and so sad come Sunday evening, when he would have to return. I still think it was a complete waste of time him being sent there. But asides I think that was where he had an occasion to sample 'pot' for the first time. How wicked.

We therefore had to exist as a family on Alan's state disability benefit. Back then, early '70's, the Carers Allowance was not in force. One was supposed to care out of duty. Yes, this is a true story - I can recall one day having to look in my purse to see if I had enough money to buy a loaf of bread.

In February 1972 came more sorrow. My sister's husband had died suddenly from a heart attack. This had shocked everyone; he was only 52. Alan had remarked that despite his crippled life he could still wake up in the morning and see his children. A lot of the next few months were spent consoling her.

As the months went by Alan was determined to stand and with assistance, climb the stairs. The physios as Stoke had done a marvellous job during his 9 months hospitalisation, endeavouring to make any improvement on his physical abilities. He was still severely handicapped on his discharge.

As his brain started to find other pathways to his legs, and his body had gained strength, with enormous effort, he was able to 'weight bear'. This only with crutches, specially adapted with a wrist plate welded on. (He had no wrist extensors – because his spinal cord had been damaged above C6, this ability to lift the wrist backwards or forwards had become non-existent.) Then a strap to buckle the crutch to his hands, because he had no grip. Then using the standing transfer lift – Voila he was up on his feet. Many a time we would cry "don't lose the strap", without the straps holding his hand to the crutches he was scuppered. I remember one time going into a shop and asking for "a leather strap to strap my husband's hand to his crutch" as the words left my mouth, I realised how ludicrous this sounded!!! Fifty shades of grey......!

The next major hurdle was to tackle the stairs. He had been sleeping downstairs in the dining room with all the ablutions also being performed in this room. This included using the commode, bed bath, urine drainage attached and dressed. We had two young children that would have friends into play, they could not understand why this room was out of bounds, so to climb the stairs and sleep in his own bedroom was vital. We had a beautiful cherry tree outside the bedroom window. I had said to Alan, you must be upstairs to see the wonderful blossom in the spring. So that was the next 'mountain' to climb. The physio from Stoke had said you will never manage stairs, so be resigned to the fact you will have to move. He proved her wrong!! So, with a rail fitted on the wall, and one person in front, holding his hand on to the rail and another behind, placing his feet on the stairs, and pushing. He saw his bedroom for the first time in months. I should point out that the first attempt ended with Alan on the floor because the incompetent person who fitted the rail had not secured it properly and it had pulled off the wall!

It wasn't until some years later we had the bathroom adapted for his needs. This included installing a shower, which he used to wallow in. The original separate toilet and bathroom were knocked into one large room. So much more accessible for Alan.

Previously the nurses had refused to get him into the bath, so he had to have bed baths. Can you imagine having to have someone else removing the faeces, and the resultant mess your bum was in at the end? I remember, at times, getting into the bath with him, squatting down, arms round him and a big heave ho to get him upright, swung round onto a chair. Make sure brakes were on.

He used to so enjoy his shower. Perhaps a mundane thing for us, but such a cleansing pleasure for him. Alan had discovered a shower at Little Comfort Farm - the 'holiday' home we found in Devon. He was now able to stand/sit in the cubicle and be completely cleansed from top to tail. The onerous task of trying to get him into a bath was no longer necessary.

All this progress took months if not years. Throughout all this he was to remain doubly incontinent and sexually impotent, until the end of his days.

From the day of his accident, I had had to take over the driving, which I hated and still do. So next motivation was to tackle driving and getting a specially adapted car. It was amazing all the levers, knobs, and super dooper power boost, that was needed. All the bells and whistles fitted, all self-funded and designed at great cost. Then Alan was behind the wheel again. He used to say, once behind the wheel, I am as good as the next man. No quarters given!

Caring for Alan had become 2nd nature to me. It was not easy to find nurses to get Alan up and perform all the necessary duties to get him down stairs to face another day. This would take about 3 hours. To begin with we had nurses call for just two mornings a week. I was always getting Alan to bed and be on duty weekends and Christmas, and bank holidays., i.e., 365 days a year. This would mean that at Christmas the children would have to wait patiently until I had got Alan downstairs at about 11a.m before they could open their presents. It was something they had to respect. We did strive over the years to keep as normal as possible family lifestyle. Both having their separate 'first days at school'.

Gavin had to become Man of the House - mowing the lawn, cycling down to the High Street to get fresh rolls from the bakery for Saturday tea - this at about 8 years old.

Gavin had joined the cubs. One night it was very foggy, so I walked down the road to meet him. There he was coming up on his bicycle. He gave me a lift home on the cross bar! Of course, there were the normal childhood ailments. Chicken pox, mumps etc. also hospital visits. Lorna, at 4 years younger than Gavin, would try copying her older brother. One day she fell out of the tree that Gavin was climbing. Gash on her head. I put her onto Alan's lap, (his shirt was covered in blood) whilst I got ready to take her to the hospital. She had 3 stitches. Another time she was playing in a friend's garden, they carried her back home with her teeth sticking out like lumps of seaside rock. She had tried climbing onto a disused sink unit and it had toppled over on top of her. Trip to the dental hospital. I was almost pleased it had happened outside of our home; I was beginning to think I was a neglectful parent! It transpired that Lorna was very accident prone. We later bought her a pony and all the ensuing accidents. See anon.

Another time Gavin had been tripped up at school and his front tooth had been chipped. More dental hospital visits. Also, Gavin had to be circumcised, another hospital to be introduced to. All this as a 'single parent', Alan having to stay at home worrying. Yes, you could say life was full on.

One day an ex-boyfriend turned up on the doorstep. Someone I had known some 9 years ago. He was a Hungarian wrestler, so very athletic. I asked him if he would teach Gavin to swim. I hated the water, still do. This wasn't the reason he had got back in touch, and he soon disappeared off the scene. I think Alan was concerned that I would up sticks and run off with him. No way – Alan was my beloved.

COMPENSATION

It became obvious that Alan was never going to earn a living. So, thoughts turned to gaining compensation for Alan's injuries from his employer. This was to take 5years from the date of his injury. Times were very trying, existing on state benefits. Also, given our two growing children, some of the other things that their school mates were being given, were completely out of reach for us to give them. At one stage I contracted pleurisy because of all the stress. I was extremely poorly for several weeks. I remember having to drag myself out of bed every morning to try to face another day. A wonderful district nurse, Irene, was caring for Alan in the morning, and with the help of Joyce, got the two children dressed ready for school, one or other of them would walk them down to school. Or sometimes even big brother Gavin took his sister down to the school. Eventually they found an antibiotic that seemed to do the trick. I remember one tea time, dear Joyce brought me a tray of food, including cold baked beans. It was all so delicious. I hadn't eaten hardly anything for weeks. Somehow or other, the children were given their tea and got put to bed. Gavin had always been very capable, and now Lorna had to be 'quite grown up'.

So, five years since the accident, it was to culminate in Alan being awarded record damages in The Supreme Court of Judicature High Court of London, Thursday 4th July 1974, our 10th wedding anniversary. So, Alan had won the highest damages in the country. This was despite the defendants called upon Brent and Harrow Area Health Authority witnesses to say they would be responsible for Alan's future nursing care, thereby reducing the nursing cost claim. This was to be another 'fight' with the NHS many years later. Also, they took on board the doctor's prognosis from Stoke Mandeville who had stated that Alan should be expected to live for another 20 years only. Thereby calculating his needs down to x 20 years. The amount awarded today would be in the region of £9 million!

The barrister was Oliver Popplewell, now Lord Chief Justice Popplewell. The first barrister Alan had dismissed as being useless, and not understanding the complexity of the case. Alan had done most of the research regarding quantum himself. The defendants had denied liability, right up until at the doors of the court. Our barrister insisted they were liable as it was due to the firm's negligence in not ensuring that the right moving equipment was to be used, that the accident had occurred. They had relented and agreed for the case to be heard at the last minute. They had called upon Professor Sir Ludwig Gutttman as their expert witness. Ludwig was the instigator of getting Stoke Mandeville renowned as THE hospital for spinal injuries in the world. This was a big bonus for us as the professor had been round to visit us at home and knew exactly how very badly Alan had been injured. He was a lovely man, not much bigger than me (I am only 4'7") It was quite ironic that later his wife was to suffer a spinal injury. The judge cleared the court of young people because the case was of a delicate nature. The judge was astounded on hearing that Alan had to have a condom glued to his penis 24/7. Alan had to swear on the bible at the hearing. I remember Alan's hands went into spasm and the court clerk had to unwrap his fingers from around the bible!

IRENE.

What a dear, dear nurse she was. She had nursed at a specialist hospital in Ireland and was now living in this country. She was the only one that Lorna let cut her toe nails! She would tell us that she could not cope if whilst not in uniform there was any incident involving blood. Dear Irene, volunteered to be a witness, at Alan's case for damages in the High Court of London. No mean feat for anyone to appear before such eminent judges. Bless you Irene.

BETTER TIMES

We were both so overjoyed and relieved to at long last have some money to spend. We had a lovely party with all the wonderful people that had been so supportive over the last 5 years.

Alan bought a brand spanking new Volvo estate car, that we could all pile into with crutches wheelchair kids etc. Alan had progressed to walking a few steps with crutches, and after lots of failed attempts was able to climb the stairs, with crutches strapped on and some one behind him giving a push on his bottom and then placing one foot at a time on the tread, reaching the summit as he called it. The reverse procedure brought him down, facing backwards. His legs were to be stronger than his arms and hands. An "upside-down paraplegic" as someone remarked. The crutches had to be adapted because of non-existent wrist flexor. Metal plates were welded onto the back of the crutches to hold his wrist upright and a leather strap threaded round his hand and buckled at the front. It used to be a case of 'don't lose the strap' - seriously because without the crutches strapped to his hand, he would be unable to use them.

Then came a glorious holiday in Portugal. We were able to afford a male nurse to come with us. This allowed me to have a 'care' free holiday also. We met a lovely family called the Windsors. No not them.........

Alan always dreamed of buying a villa in Portugal. It was not to be.......

It was around this time that we had a two-storey side extension put onto the side of the house. This was to be a large 4th bedroom upstairs and a garage and adjoining utility room downstairs accessed from the kitchen. The landing upstairs had the window there made into a doorway to the bedroom.

During all this building work we had retreated to our 'haunt' in Devon. Again, Joyce was to oversee the builders. I remember her shock upon going into our dining room, to find all the workmen sitting around the bath having lunch. "You do realise they are due home tomorrow!" she said. The whole house was a mess. The final knock through from the house into the new extension they just managed to complete before we arrived back from Devon!

We had found a lovely self-catering holiday cottage in Devon in 1971. It was ideal. All on one floor and with an en-suite bedroom with a shower. This was the first time Alan had experienced the ease of a shower. He was determined to get one at home. The district nurses refused to get him into the bath at home. This was a worry because his skin viability had to remain clean and dry.

I would load us all up and drive us down to Braunton and Little Comfort Farm. Before the days of the dual carriageway. Just the old A30. It was lovely there and the kids were able to play in the stream with the owner's children. I must admit to being very tired - driving, cooking and caring for Alan and Gavin and Lorna. But it had to be done for the family unit. Gavin suffered from asthma and despite the medication one year he was very poorly. This was when I realised what good people who owned the cottage were. Mrs Alvsaker (Nims) was a nurse and took Gavin off to the doctors, whilst I was getting Alan up and dressed. The first year of my sister becoming a widow, we took her and her son with us on holiday. Not any easy time trying to keep her cheerful. But the kids had a good time.

I remember we spent a lovely evening on the burrows there eating fish and chips from the newspaper.

Later my sister was to move up to Sheffield to live with one of her husband comrades from the war. He was also windowed, so an ideal arrangement.

Horse riding. Yes, thought Alan, I'll try that. He was so determined to 'make the very best of a very bad job' We all went to Suzanne's riding school in Stanmore, only to be told the chap that ran the Riding for the Disabled, had recently suffered a stroke, and was still recovering. Lorna had always hankered after a pony. "Might my daughter have some children's lessons then", asked her dad. The next week saw Lorna off to have her first riding lesson. That was to be the beginning of her lifetime with horses.

We also had 2 good friends, Bern and Pauline. Bern had known Alan longer than me; they were teenagers together and shared a love of motor bikes. These folks ran a Church of England children's home, Twizzletwig. They kindly would take our 2 children to stay with them. Great fun was to be had in the log cabins and zip wires built by Bern in the surrounding woods. This also gave Alan and myself a 'breather'. We remain good friends still, 50 years later.

After 1974 and post compensation, we had been to Braunton and were driving home and we both looked at one another and simultaneously said "why are we going back to the rat race?" Alan wasn't working and there was nothing to keep us in Harrow. This started a long whole year of searching for suitable property in Devon. We would leave the children with my dear neighbour Joyce or Alan's mother and come down to Devon on a mission. We stayed at a motel attached to a pub. This was to later become Jethros, the comedian's abode. We had a list of specifications of houses we were looking for. We were then to realise what a large county Devon was! Armed with all the estate agent's details of possible houses, we would set off for the weekend. It would mainly be a case of we would draw up outside and immediately drive off or I would be sent into do a 'recce' to see if it might be a possibility. It was too much effort to get Alan out of car and into the property if it was a "no go". One time we ended up after a long drive down an overgrown drive to an enormous house. We had just pulled up when some old local stuck his head in Alan's window and informed us "I got buggering shingles ain't I!". Can still hear him uttering those words even today. Anyway, I went in to do my usual 'recce' The big oak door slammed behind me. Ooo er I thought. Bit creepy. It must have been a beautiful grand house at one time. Upon going into one room there was a pile of nesting material on the floor by the fireplace. "Buggering Jackdaws", I was informed again. The rooms were empty of any furniture. We then proceeded down a corridor and downs some steps to the kitchen. Huge room.

But I realised this would not be the one for us, too large, too much refurbishment needed and rather remote. I quickly thanked him and made my escape. We never could remember where this house was.

It was nearly a year later and we had almost giving up of finding 'our' house. But that Saturday morning another agent's details came through the post. It was an old rectory, that had just come onto the market. It looked a bit interesting.

MOVING TO THE COUNTRY

We drove up to the rectory. Yes, it had possibilities. Drove past and around the corner up the lane. Pulled into a gateway and looked back. WOW this was it! I went and had a look inside. The rector's wife was very glum and unwelcoming. But despite it being very old fashioned and needing an update, it definitely had possibilities. We went back to the agents and made them an offer. No, it was, on the Church of England's instruction, to go to auction. Another drama.

We went home and started to find out all about buying property at auction. The following weekend was to see us again viewing the property. This time Alan came in and also met Mrs. Grumpy. We later were to learn that she did not want to move. The Church was 'kicking them out'!

Alan saw the possibilities. All wide doors, no steps downstairs. There were also 2 staircases, so if the time came and Alan would not be able to manage stairs, we could take the secondary stairway out and have a lift fitted. This 2nd stairs were in fact for the maid's use; there were in "yee olden days" 2 maids. The whole house was arranged whereby servants would not have to come into direct contact with the rector and his family. We even discovered call bells in the loft!

Outside the grounds were all level, an unusual thing to find in Devon! It was normally out the door and either up a hill or down one.

But still Alan had not inspected upstairs. There were 5 bedrooms and 2 bathrooms. The bathroom leading off the main bedroom was small but I hoped usable by Alan.

We had had a survey taken on the house and no horrible nasties came to light. The surveyor did say it would need some modernisation. For example, there was just one power point in the kitchen!

THE AUCTION

It was 24th November 1976, 7 years since the accident. Alan and I went into the pub in Holsworthy where the auction was to be held – upstairs! Folks carried Alan up the stairs. A lovely Devonian gent had bought Alan a beer.

The auction started. It had nearly reached our limit before Alan had put his hand up. It had stalled and the auctioneer was saying "go on sir, you'll lose it!" A chap behind was also urging Alan on. We later discovered this was to be our new neighbour. Trevor Box, a very typical Devonian farmer. I was also nudging him on. The hammer went down. We had bought a dilapidated rectory in rural Devon!

We were very fortunate to have a friend of a friend, Les, who said he would take on the task of renovating the old rectory. This "Les' was in fact Leslie Isted. Hence our house is now called Isted House. In honour of all the time and hard work he put into the work on the property. Part of the sale contract was that we had to rename the house. This was to become our home for the next 40plus years. Les moved in in April and lived there, or rather camped there! It did need a lot of modernising!

We had sold our 4-bedroom property in Harrow and we were anxious to move. Both children were about to move into senior and junior schools that September, so July 1977 saw us up sticks and move, lock stock and barrel. Les had been working tirelessly for 3 months. Alan's bedroom and adapted bathroom was complete. The rest of the house was like living on a builder's site. We had a wonderful solid fuel Rayburn in the kitchen. That was our main source of cooking and heating. Good old Les had been busy chopping logs as well. The grounds were surrounded by trees, so a wonderful source for logs. The house is still stood amidst some wonderful specimens of oak, ash and beech etc.

We managed to arrange district nurses to come and get Alan up, which could take up to 3 hours, but only for 2 mornings a week. The other mornings and every evening I was the duty 'nurse'. I still have the note the first nurse wrote on her 1st morning.

 "Young man with his 2 children and wife. Starting a new life. Severely crippled but also very determined".

Mayers – first house visit from doc

"Where's all the money come from?", he said. We were both shocked to hear him say this. So unprofessional. A) nothing to do with him B) not relevant to the patient doc situation. How can a professional medical man ask such a question? Yes, we now live in a large beautiful house in the countryside, with glorious views. Neither here nor there as to whether he should be concerned.

One of our first purchases was a Simplicity ride on mower, with a tiller attached at the rear. Not only was this Alan's legs for getting about outside, but also mowing the grass. He even tilled and made a vegetable patch. It was to be a constant few words in our vocabulary – NO SUCH THING AS CAN'T - 'NSTAC'!

The modus operandum of getting Alan onto the ride on was thus, haul him onto his feet from the wheelchair, swivel round to the vehicle seat, lower onto seat. Then pass one leg over steering wheel, as if breaking a wish bone (and make a wish) and then place right food onto accelerator pedal, on for go and off for stop. Turn engine on for him, engage gear and off he could go! Someone would have to engage mower or tiller, and then again, someone to empty grass cutting bucket. He was so pleased to be able to do something. NSTAC! Many times someone would have to go and find him and rescue him from the out back!!

We tried very hard to fit in with the locals and not to bring our "towney" ways to their country ways. Trevor, our neighbour, was constantly amused by my cockney slang! Also, I was 'mazed' at some of their words.

Lorna walked up to the local school with her friends. The school was just about ½ mile away. Gavin was quite surprised that he had a bus journey to go to the senior school which was about 13 miles away.

Gavin made friends with Andrew a boy of the same age, who lived in the village. They made a marvellous tree house in our orchard. I remember Andrew peering in the kitchen window, Alan was outside at the time, and he said to Andrew "what are you looking at?" "There's a fire in the kitchen" he replied! I had forgotten to take all of the packaging from the new oven. Quickly extinguished and no harm done.

There was an old cider orchard in one of the fields. This was so old and dying that we had it cleared. I never did get to see it before it was all sawn down - so busy coping with other things indoors. But we had a marvellous Guy Fawkes Bonfire Night that autumn, with Les building the fire and making a huge guy. We invited the neighbours - not a huge crowd. The house was, in those days in splendid isolation.

Alan had American relatives. His Aunt was a G I bride. Her and one of her sons had flown over to see her sister, Alan's mother. They wanted to come and see us in our new home. At that stage it was still waiting on more modernisation. i.e., not always having electricity and rooms still waiting to be decorated. At the same time Les had gone to Trevor to help with the harvest. Those were the days before big contractors came with their state-of-the-art machinery to do the job in a much shorter time. So, the day before the American connection arrived, we had no electricity! Difficult trying to clean, hoover, and cook with no electrics! Also, most of the rooms were only fit for camping in!

I remember Aunty saying "Gee, you've got grass growing on the trees." Of course, this was lichen. We were already familiarising ourselves with the country! They all admired our new abode. I think Alan's mum thought we were mad. Huge house, away from her and her sons (Alan had 4 brothers).

She told me we would never manage. Of course, she was proved wrong….

In 1981 it was the 'Year of the Disabled. Alf Morris was at the time Minister for the Disabled. Alan was approached as to whether he would open the annual Playing Fields Gala. He was delighted to do so. A good day was had by all. Alan gave a very good speech, and Lorna ran the pony rides with her pony Nimble. We were almost getting accepted by the locals! Forty years later and still foreigners! Albeit, we are now the longest standing residents in the hamlet!

Several years later people still remember this event.

Another 'incident' was when Lorna and Nimble came a cropper. Nimble was Lorna's second pony of her own. Lorna had come off, Nimble had trod on her toe whilst scrambling to get up. The outcome was her toe was dislocated. Gavin had to carry her into the car. Then followed a trip to hospital in Barnstaple (80 odd mile round trip!), plaster and crutches.

Another year the Church asked if they could use our grounds to hold the annual church fete. We said we would be delighted. The weather was good and we met up with even more local folks.

Trevor, our neighbour living opposite, was on the local parish council committee and he would take Alan with him, just out of interest, and to meet other locals. One evening, I thought I could smell burning. I opened the door of the fitted wardrobe (good old Les had made this) - Yes definitely a smell of burning. Phoned 999. I said I just want some advice I think I can smell burning. Within 10 minutes we had 3 fire engines here and dozens of firemen. Meanwhile Trevor's wife had phoned the pub, (by this time the meeting had finished and they were ensconced there) and told the publican there's a fire down here. Trevor bundled Alan into the car and they made all haste back. It turned out to be a chimney fire. Not serious, but the crew waited until the inspector had arrived from Barnstaple. All very efficient.

Today our plumber Gary Allcorn, is a retained firefighter and son of the fireman attending that night.

The next year Alan thought he would buy some young bullocks from market. It seemed a good idea at the time. Alan enjoyed watching their progress and fattening. The time came for them to be sent to market. All very successful. Next year, same thing. But this time they were a rogue bunch! They kept breaking out. At one stage we had all the local farmers trying to catch them. They rampaged into the neighbour's vegetable patch. Eventually ending up at a farm about 5 miles away! Alan had sat at the window watching helplessly. NEVER AGAIN he vowed!

Another time we went to a local auction and bought a toboggan. "You won't have much use for that" said Gordon Millar, the auctioneer. "We don't have snow in this part of the country." He was wrong!! That winter we were snowed in! Which meant also no electricity. I went outside with my camera to take some photos of the blizzard, but soon retreated indoors. Very scary. The next day the snow was up to hedge height. We sent the 2 children up to the village to get a refill gas canister for the fire, with the aforementioned sleigh. Goodness knows what Gordon and Jackie, owners of the garage, thought when they saw 2 children appear dragging the sleigh down the main road. We welcomed the children back with open arms. We could now have a fire in the sitting room. The good old solid fuel Aga was being a 'mother' to the rest of the house. The next day the children and I were commandeered by Trevor to follow him into the fields. We were each issued with long canes. The idea being we were to plunge these into the ground, in an attempt to locate any sheep buried there. We later heard of friends in the nearby village, going for a walk in the snow. They became completely disorientated and were looking for the chapel land mark. They suddenly realised they were standing ON the chapel roof!

The children were to have great fun toboggining down the snow-covered field and lanes. We got Alan onto the ride on mower, Gavin hitched the sleigh onto the back, and they all went for a ride round the house. Then the next day Alan thought he would like to have a go on the sleigh - 'NSTAC'. Between us we got him onto the sleigh and Gavin started pushing him down the field. Lorna was sat on the back holding him on, but he toppled off into the snow. Zac, our Labrador dog, thought it was great fun, licking master's face! Mainly with Gavin's help, he was now 12 and getting a strong boy, we got Alan back on the sleigh, and with Gavin driving the ride on mower, trundled back up to the house.

Someone thought it would be a good idea to write and make a film. I had a super eight video camera. It was the size of a small suitcase to take around. Anyway, the film depicted a robbery. We duly parked outside Lloyds Bank in Holsworthy, one dismal Sunday afternoon. I stood taking shots outside the bank. It is a wonder the local bobby did pop up to ask what we were doing. Another film making escapade was a burglary at home. Lorna playing the little girl mugged. Gavin playing the villain and of course Alan as Ironside in his wheelchair. Probably sounds very infantile. But we enjoyed performing this as our small troupe of four! Then Gavin's mates wanted to have a try. So off they went across the fields on a various assortment of pushbikes and scrambler bikes, chasing some baddies. Forgotten now who was behind the camera!

We had now bought a dog, Zac a black Labrador. What a clown he was! Gavin took to taking him to dog shows, with great success, which was surprising as when we went to view the litter of puppies, Zac was the last one and 'runt' of the litter. At an early dog show when the breeder saw Gavin showing Zac, he really liked the dog and wanted to buy him back. No way, we couldn't part with our 'clown' The next year we bought yellow bitch Gen. She was bought on the recommendation of a top breeder. But did not have the success that Zac had had.

In 1993 Zac and Gen were PTS. It was, I thought, very lonely without any animals. Alan couldn't understand this, when as he said we had horses in the stable. Anyway, Lorna wanted a dalmatian. We duly went off to find our Dotty the dally. After a couple of years, I thought it would be nice to have some puppies. They were pure joy, but oh my, selling them was a torture. Joe public seemed to have no idea about owning a puppy. One, a taxi driver phoned to say he would have one of the puppies. He had a fair to go to in London. Would pick the puppy up, then go on to the fair in London and asked if he would need a dish for his food! Unbelievable! Of course, I said no, you are not having one of my puppies. I was pleased to say all the puppies ended up in wonderful loving homes. The owners would keep me informed of their progress and ultimately of their demise. Happy days.

The children were enjoying country life. We had bought Gavin an old scrambler motorbike. He and his friend had much enjoyment riding round the fields. Although a lot of the time the bike was in pieces on the garage floor. Then there was scrambler meeting locally. Poor Gavin's bike was still in pieces, but a smashing chap, called Dave Cholwill, let Gavin borrow his. How kind! Other people, who were to become some very good friends, were Ian Drowne and his wife Pauline. Pauline worked as a nurse at the local village hospital, and she was one of a team who would come in the morning to get Alan up and ready for another day. Ian very generously let Gavin borrow his radio-controlled plane. Ian would fix Alan's car with several versions of devices to be strapped onto Alan's hands, enabling him to hold onto the steering wheel of his car. These dear people were the first 'locals, to accept us into their lives.

Gavin attended a course at North Devon College. He was late getting back one night, so I decided to drive out to look for him. I found a moped going along a country lane in the dark. Thinking it was Gavin I stopped the car. The poor young girl driving the moped must have had a fright. "Very sorry" I said, "I thought you were my son!"

Then came Gavin's 18th Birthday. It was going to be a big surprise. Alan had arranged for him to have a flying lesson at a local aerodrome. Gavin still hadn't guessed as we were driving along the A30, where we were exactly going. Only when we drove into the place and he saw several light aircraft, did he realise. This was October, and after taking off the fog arrived. He was to later tell us the only way they found their way back to land was to follow the A30.

Also round about this time Gavin was to become an advanced motorcyclist. How proud were his mum and dad!?

RESPITE

There was no respite for me for several years, until we had been living in Devon for a while. The suggestion was made, can't remember from whom, a stay at Rowans, might be beneficial. Goodness what a lovely place that was. Just for young disabled people. Geared for the young person in mind. So many times disabled would be lumped with the 'diselderly. Most depressing. Several years he went there quite happily for respite. Unfortunately, after a time funds for the place were removed.

Tamar lakes.

We had got friendly with local garage owners. Gordon and Jackie Aegerter. They were keen sailors. Why not come sailing on Tamar lake suggested Gordon? Alan being the go getter he was, was very keen to give it a go. With help from club members to rig and launch the boat and numerous hands to get Alan on board, Gordon provided tuition and assistance to Alan, by riding on the outrigger, and off they would sail.

Alan once said to me 'I wish I had your strength' but goodness me, my dearest, you had so much determination and fortitude This is what he had to have for the continuation of his life, until the end.

SIA

An organisation that we found very useful was the Spinal Injuries Association. Founded in 1974, by Founder and President Baroness Masham of Ilton, who became spinal cord injured at T5 following a riding accident in 1958. The first director of the SIA Stephen Bradshaw, lived quite locally to us whilst we lived in London and often came for tea and cake. He worked tirelessly for the organisation and was awarded an O.B.E.

Our lives jogged along for about 12 years, and then our neighbour Trevor and his wife Mavis decided to sell the farm and move. He sold it to 'The Neighbour from Hell'! There was to follow 6 years of this horrid person. He would deliberately trespass and cause criminal damage to our property with his tractor and other machines. Numerous occasions we had to call the police, even they were getting angry with this man's attitude. In the end, he had to appear at the magistrates' court, and he was bound him over to keep the peace, in the sum of £2000, for 2 years. We also reported our case to the local government ombudsman. They went on to find the county highways guilty of maladministration and fined them £5000. The highways had become involved because they had insisted that the land in question was "highway", therefore the neighbour had every right to drive over and cause incredible damage to the land and leaving the tarmacked road covered in mud and dangerous to other road users. Even though our deeds showed this land to be in our possession. The law stated that land outside hedge banks is deemed high ways. Although this particular 'highway' had large trees growing on it. The ombudsman fined them for 'dithering' over several years as to if it was actually highway. So, they were allowing the neighbour to cause incredible damage to land and road, by their ineptitude. This said person died and then the authority decided that they didn't want the so called 'highway' anyway. We then duly signed a stopping up order. That was the end of 7 years of miserable wonderings of what trouble he would cause next.

Back to the children:

Lorna had joined the Young Farmers. She had quite a lot of success in the debating team, travelling to Exeter for the finals. The team were very successful under the tutelage of a prominent local farmer Jeff Endacott.

Gavin had left school and was able to get an apprenticeship at the dockyard in Plymouth, this mainly because of the outbreak of the Falklands war, and Maggie wanted more battleships built. He was now living in digs in Plymouth. Yes, he did survive, even though I, his Mum thought he wouldn't! He joined a Karate club and went on to achieve his black belt. As previously mentioned, he was to become an advanced motorist. This was done at the age of 18! At 19 he had a computer programme published and sold it! Very proud of what my son had aspired to despite not having a physically able-bodied dad. Then when he came home for the weekends, he would give driving lessons, in Okehampton, on Saturday morning, to learner drivers on their motorcycles. Then the dock yard had lots of rumours about the lack of incoming contracts to build ships. The rumours were to lead on to threats of redundancy. So, Gavin decided to leave and go for a degree in computing at Plymouth University. He succeeded in getting a 1st degree and started looking again for work. This is when he ended up moving to Cheltenham. He met Jo, and they eventually got married on the London Eye. It was magical. We obviously drove up to London VERY early that morning. Lorna's then partner, did the driving. Got a bit lost doing the scenic tour round Buckingham Palace. We arrived at the

London Marriott County Hall hotel. We were greeted by Gavin, saying they had had to stop the "wheel" as it was frozen. This was in January, so perhaps not surprising. There then followed an anxious wait to hear whether the ceremony was to go ahead. With a couple of hours before the due time we were told, yes, it is 'go'. It was very exciting. The wedding party, including Alan in his wheelchair, were just ushered on board, leaving all the plebs in the queue. As the wheel reached 12 o'clock, the happy couple said "I do". It was beautiful walking over Westminster bridge with us all in full 'bridal' outfits, complete with bridal bouquet. That evening we all went out for a meal at a recommended restaurant. Gavin's now brother-in-law is in the Metropolitan police, so knew of the best place to go. We spent the night at the hotel, and the next morning, said goodbye and went our separate ways home. He is now living in a lovely 4 bedroomed house in Cheltenham with his wife Jo, and my grandson Barry. As I write this, I am informed, that Barry has just been voted 'sportsman of the year' at his school - clever lad! He so excels at ALL sports. His grandad would have been so proud. Barry now swims for his county.

Lorna had finished her A levels and went off to university to obtain a degree in Biology and Chemistry.

Lorna had only agreed to move with us to the country on the condition she could have a pony. This we did. Big mistake! The owners assured us it was a 1st pony. The pony was called Sherry and if she couldn't buck Lorna off, she would take her under trees and knock her off! Lorna went around Holsworthy show (our local agricultural show) one year with black eyes! But this didn't deter her. Along came Nimble. What a treasure. Her confidence grew. We found a good instructor Keri. We came back one day, to be told by Lorna, Sherry bucked and I stayed on! Lorna joined the local branch of The Pony Club, an organisation I thoroughly can recommend! It teaches the children so much about how to care for their ponies, having to think about another living creature as well as themselves. Of course, there were all the competitions to be entered and won. Lorna riding Nimble would tear round the cross-country courses, loving it and winning. I think she has inherited my competitive streak and Alan's sense of adventure. (Alan had always said the best day of his life was riding his brother's motor cycle round the track at Brands Hatch). Then we bought a bigger pony called

Starry. The owners, Mr. Mrs. Tomlin, were so kind, they offered us their horse trailer to bring Starry home in. A super genuine pony that would jump anything but had the unruliest mane. Lorna and Starry went on to win the pony club camp show jumping cup 3 years running, moving up the age grades. This really made many members a bit disgruntled. Then came Sefton, a very showy 14.2 pony. He had come from a showing home, but Lorna soon showed him the fun of jumping. He was really a small thoroughbred pony. So very different from the scruffy ponies Lorna had had previously. But he was a good precursor to the next horse to join our yard. The legendary Touch of Gold!!

MOVING ON UP IN THE HORSE WORLD.

Sue Willcocks had competed Touch of Gold (Tache) up to advanced Horse Trials. In 1980 she competed with him at Badminton. That was ultimate goal at the time and she had decided after this to do a world trip. Of course, the owners Jack and Cynthia (Sues father and mother) were looking for a new rider as Tache was still only 13 years old. He had already gone on loan to someone but was sent home as too naughty! Mrs Gilkinson, a very renowned and respected dressage judge, had suggested to the owners Lorna as a potential new rider. At this stage they were both aged fourteen.

Jack the owner came to inspect our premises, where his beloved horse might be moving to. Then we had to go down to their stables and Lorna was given the 'Spanish inquisition treatment'. Testing to see if they approved of her. And then, once more to have an actual ride on Tache. The day came and Jack brought Tache up to us in his trailer. He was very emotional. I told him he would have a loving home with us. Proving my point when the horse was to be with us for the next 19 years!

Lorna was just coming off ponies and Tache had just come down from International level eventing - a rather dauting combination!! Lorna had a few very hairy moments going around a cross country course. Tache wanted to go at 'grown up' speed. Lorna was still use to pony express! But his super movement was breath taking. They would nearly always be placed 1st in any dressage competitions. Then as the months went by, their show jumping and cross-country efforts gelled and they would then win or nearly always win the competition – whether, dressage, show jumping or eventing. They went on to win year after year at the Pony Club area trials. The other riders would groan when they saw Lorna and Tache. "Oh, it's that horse with the black spot on his bum!" Tache had a very distinctive black mark about 6"' across on his right hind quarter. They went on to qualify for many championships around the country, also taking the rest of the team with them. One year, Gill Watson the European junior event team trainer, asked Lorna do a trial up country. This was in the depth of winter for 4 days. We had now obtained an American motor home, 'Harvey' (nickname for RV – recreational vehicle as they're called across the pond!). We would hitch up a horse trailer on the back, drag and push Alan up into the driver's seat, place his hand on the controls and be all set to start. NSTAC! There was an onboard shower and toilet, equipped for Alans use. Unfortunately, early one Sunday morning, someone forgot to put the boarding steps up, and going to drive through the gate and we got them well and truly wedged on the granite gate post! This is where our wonderful friend Gordon Aegerter from the garage, came down at 6 am to disentangle us! So eventually we got to Gill Watsons yard, along with the other hopefuls. Everything was frozen including all the outside taps. Luckily the gas heater was working in the Harvey. Alan did not get out of this for 5 days until we eventually arrived back in Devon. She was chosen to go for further trial, but her father and I decided that her school work must come first. One time I said to her father "we seem to have dragged Tache all-round the country", "no" he replied, "he had dragged us all over the place!" But my goodness he certainly taught Lorna to become a very tactful rider. You didn't tell Tache, you just had to ask him please – even then he could be disinclined to cooperate! Many a top trainer that decided to try out Tache were made to look silly. He would NOT be told!

Lorna was now given the ride on Ted. A 16'3 TB x Irish draught. The owner's son had moved away, and they were looking for a rider. Lorna took Ted on. They had lots of success at eventing competitions. Ted was already competing well at show jumping by the son. Lorna's first love was eventing, so off they went. He was very genuine, and would always jump clear. Then one day, the owners were on holiday. Lorna wanted to have one last outing before the end of season. TOG and Ted were both entered at the local Ashbury hunter trial. Ted went well. Then it was Tache's round. As it was a hunter trial and not a horse trial, there was on the course a hunting gate. This had to be opened and shut whilst still on board. But of course, Tache, being Tache, would not stop for anything once he had started his round. Lorna could feel that he was getting set to jump the gate. She was trying desperately to pull him off course. He just clipped the fence, and they both went tumbling down the hill. The ambulance was called. Everyone rushed to Lorna's aid, including the hunt master. He kicked his horse to go to Lorna's side, his horse bucked and sent him flying! The onlookers stopped. They didn't know which way to go – to Lorna, or the hunt master, also on the floor. At the hospital, the doctors were worried that she might have broken her pelvis. But after some anxious wait for X-rays, no, all clear. Lorna had to stay overnight in the hospital for observation. Poor Gavin had got cajoled into driving Lorna and the two horse to the event. Lorna was too young to drive the owners 7.5.t lorry. "We shan't be long", we told Gavin. Gavin was not the least bit interested in the horse scene. After Lorna's accident, the poor lad had to load to horses on to the lorry, drive them home and then unload them and put them in their stables. Lorna was to turn up the following morning. Oh, the joys of horses…

NOW BACK TO DEAR ALAN

There were times when Alan would just retreat 'back into himself', in his own world. There was nothing I could do or say, just leave him for a while. Couple of hours later and he would be back in our world.

We had purchased a 2nd hand through floor lift. The first one also 2nd hand had to be discarded. It was a manually operated, and to get from one floor to the next, I had to turn a large wheel to move the lift up. I don't know who was more incapacitated when Alan had arrived on the first floor, him or me! So, we now had this mechanical lift. Old but usable. Alan would be stood from his wheelchair by a carer and then walk a couple steps into the lift. For some reason this night, Alan's shoes had been taken off. This unfortunately led to Alan having a spasm, the stimuli from Alan's foot on the floor without shoes caused this and Alan landed in a heap on the floor of the lift. Ambulance time again. When he arrived at RDE hospital, the staff all thought he was very brave by not crying out in pain. Alan's condition made his broken ankle painless. We had to go back the next day for the ankle to be put in plaster. This was rather concerning as the plaster may cause pressure sores.

It was quite amusing! On one visit the nurse said to us "take a seat, Oh I see you've bought your own" looking at Alan! She had not realised what a wry sense of humour we saw in this. The lift had now grown older and the concertina door had to be carefully dragged across and made sure it connected to the switch on the other side, to make the lift ascend. Eventually this switch no longer worked. A friend came down and removed this safety function. Sometimes the lift would travel up with the door open! Later this lift was to be condemned by the authorities and was not to be used. When the OT visited, I asked how was he to get upstairs to bed and the bathroom. "Oh", she said, "he must sleep downstairs and wash at the kitchen sink" This by someone confined to a wheelchair. Alan just ignored her 'good advice' and continued to use the lift at his own peril.

Alan had been prescribed an Oswestry Standing Frame by Stoke Mandeville hospital. It was a wooden contraption, about 3'x3' with a table at waist height and 2 poles about 6' high coming out from the table, down to the floor. With help, someone pushing from behind and then someone wrapping his hand onto the poles, Alan was able to stand in the frame. He was able to stand for 20-30minutes. This 'exercise' was so beneficial to all of his body, legs, bowels, and bladder function. After the broken ankle Alan could not do this vital daily exercise. So, he asked the local carpenter to build something, from Alan's design, that would enable him to stand but not put any weight on the broken ankle. I think I still have this gizmo. So, yet another hurdle overcome.

On another occasion having to make a trip to the hospital, this time with Alan driving, all the parking spaces were taken, so we parked in the hospital car spot. Upon coming back to his car, afterwards, there was a parking ticket, stuck to the vehicle. It was stuck on window out of Alan's reach. The notice stated that 'only the driver of the vehicle was to remove'. I phoned the appropriate authority mentioning the predicament. My husband is in a wheelchair and cannot reach to remove the notice. What shall he do? "Oh dear" she said "we haven't come across that question before". I do wish that able bodied people realised the difficulties of being confined to a wheelchair. I removed the notice.

The next NSTAC, was to try to get a lorry/horsebox that Alan was able to drive. The first criteria was, it had to have an automatic transmission gearbox. This proved to be extremely difficult to acquire a 7.5-ton lorry with automatic transmission (readily available nowadays.). Eventually one was found up country. Again, we called on a friend to drive it back to Devon for us. The body was unusable. We had a firm in Devon convert it into living, with a toilet area which would be suitable for Alan's use. We then set about getting the steering "light enough" for Alan to manage. But this was one time when 'no such word as can't' was not true. Alan would be fine driving along the road, but when it came to a roundabout, Lorna would have to leap across and turn the steering wheel. So, it wasn't long before Lorna was not only having to drive the lorry, but also having to compete at the horse trials.

At one event at Gatcombe Park, we took the wrong turning out of the field and ended up driving down Princess Anne's drive. Lorna said, I don't think we should be going down here. We saw all the security cameras following us, and then a policeman appeared on the drive. "I shouldn't be here" questioned Lorna. "No" said the police, and kindly escorted us back. We were stabled overnight at Princess Anne's stables. The next morning, as Lorna was getting the horse ready, Her Highness appeared and started talking to Lorna. What a lovely unpretentious person she is.

We had some fun times with that vehicle. It was a rather old one. One night coming home all the lights suddenly disappeared. Pitch black, slightly unnerving! Another time the groom who was travelling with us said "My feet are in water" in the well of the cab. Hey ho. During these forays, dear Gavin was left at home getting dad to bed. We would make special arrangements for a carer to come in on those mornings.

Another trip we broke down on the M25. We were taking a horse we had bought from Ireland and that Lorna had 'brought on', up to Cambridge. The chap had said he would like to buy him. So, there we were trugging up the motorway and suddenly nothing. Those were the days before mobile phones. The motorway cameras could see a huge traffic jam, but apparently, we were just out of the camera's view. Cars were beeping at us as though we had stopped there for fun. There was no hard shoulder because there were roadworks. Nightmare! Suddenly the rescue guy turned up, organised by the highway people. The engine had blown up. Fortunately, he towed us to his home. The first thing we saw was a horse box. Hurrah we both thought! The AA rescue plan was to get us to our destination, or back home. No way could we be towed the 100s miles back home with a horse on board. So, we off loaded, dear calm Paddy, on to the chap's horsebox. Then onto our destination in Cambridge. Off loaded Paddy again and, into the stables there. Just to finish the day off the prospective client told us he was not interested in the horse after all. What a time waster. What muggins us. The next day our knight in shining armour, the rescue chap, picked us and the lorry up and towed the lorry and us back home. We had to leave Paddy there. Later we had to hire a local horsebox transporter to bring him home, at a great expense and a horse with a leg damaged in transit on the way home, plus vets' bills. I think we learnt our lesson, never again. They can come and collect the horse if they want to buy. Throughout all of this poor Alan was wondering what was going on. We managed to phone him at the rescuer's home, to put him in the picture. Gavin and the carer had been looking after Alan. All wondering how we were getting on. On our horsey trips away at weekends, Gavin would be home from the dockyard and would put Alan to bed. This was before the days, of having any care staff in the evening.

I will mention at this stage, Gavin had been undergoing counselling re an undershot jaw. He wanted an operation to correct this. Brave lad. Eventually the operation was performed and we went to see him at the hospital. Alan and I were both surprised to see his face was unblemished. All the surgery had been performed inside his mouth. I did notice a pair of pliers at the head of his bed, I wondered what they were for. Gavin was discharged home. The next day he had tremendous nose bleed. Alan thought we ought to call the ambulance and Gavin was rushed into hospital, where they cauterised the bleed. The pliers I then realised, were to be used should he start choking on the blood, to cut the wired jaw with the pliers.

Nineteen glorious years Tache and Lorna spent together. But the day had to come – he was put peacefully to sleep and buried in our field. He and Lorna were both 33 years old. They were both just 14 when the partnership has started….

In 1995 Gavin and Lorna both left home. Gavin had been living in digs at Plymouth, but now had a job offer in Cheltenham. We were then to get involved to help Gavin move his belongings up to Cheltenham. Alan arranged to hire a box van trailer. Luckily the car had a tow hitch. So, we went to pick the vehicle up. Again, a friend helped us load Gavin's things into the van and off we went. The flat that Gavin was renting was opposite the Everyman Theatre. Alan had to drive under an archway to get into the courtyard of Gavin's flat. I went up to have a look see, very nice! Gavin unloaded all his things and we were to meet up again later for a meal; we had arranged to stay at a motel with disabled facilities. A few months later Gavin bought a 2 bedroomed town house. It was lovely going up to visit him, only problem, the house had a garage on the ground floor and then up a flight of stairs to the living accommodation and bedrooms. Somehow Gavin managed to carry dad up the flight of stairs. It was a lovely house. We had by this time purchased a caravan and this enabled us to visit, without having to worry about sleeping arrangements. Gavin would come back to the caravan with us and help me get dad to bed. Then next day we did a tour of Cheltenham. Lovely town and superb shops.

Lorna, after running a successful livery yard, decided to move home and seek pastures new. Initially taking a position as yard manager and lecturer at the newly opened equine unit at Sparsholt College in Winchester. There again, the box van trailer was hired, and the journey to Sparsholt College, Winchester, undertaken. This time though the car broke down on the A30. No battery left on the mobile. I tried to phone the RAC, but can you believe being so tiny at 4'7", I could not reach the canopy of the road side phone very well. Somehow, I got a message to the RAC. They duly arrived and towed us to the nearest garage. But this involved transferring myself and the dog onto their recovery vehicle. Yes, the dog had to come too. All this alongside the busy A30. Alan meanwhile, stayed in the car. It was impossible to get him into the high recovery vehicle. I think this was probably illegal, but there was no other option. We waited anxiously at the garage. Yes, it is fixed, - no not yet. I used the garage phone to tell Lorna what was happening and why the delay. We eventually arrived back home. The garage had advised not to undertake a long journey to Winchester. Upon arrival the recovery vehicle temporarily parked in our new neighbours drive whilst we were getting our car onto the yard and transferring Alan into his wheelchair. The nasty neighbour shouted at me to get off his drive. Some people!

Caravan Purchase

The first few that I had a look inside had ridiculously small toilet areas. No more than a cupboard. We eventually found one that had the whole of the end of the caravan taken up by the toilet/shower area and dressing room. This enabled Alan and myself to visit Gavin or Lorna, without the worry of finding disabled facilities, wherever we were to turn up. I found it a lot of hard work on these trips. Also, Alan was very tired from the driving by the time we got to our destination. Getting to a camping site. I had to unhitch, put all the stabilisers down on the caravan and then get Alan on board. Alan had invented an ingenious idea of making it possible for him to get into the caravan. He purchased a battery-operated bath seat. This was put into the caravan doorway in the 'down' position. I would transfer Alan, from his wheelchair, doing a standing transfer, swivel him round, and seat him on the bath seat. Operate it into the 'up' position. He was now sitting in the caravan. The local garage chap Gordon Aegerter, had taken off the suckers on the feet and put on castor wheels. Voila – a wheelchair in the caravan. Attending to all Alan's needs in the caravan was much more difficult than the same procedures at home. But it did mean that we were able to visit them both Gavin and Lorna.

One night I had tucked Alan up for the night. We both heard a strange noise from outside the caravan. It sounded as if some animal was trying to eat its way into the caravan. I opened the door looked out and started saying 'shoo, shoo,'. Then suddenly looked up to see fireworks in the sky. The noise we had heard was actually the sound of these going off at the The Cheltenham Festival!!

Gavin and Jo had been married for a couple of years. Jo announced at Christmas 2005 that she was pregnant. Joy all round. But then, Gavin phoned to say, there was no heart beat to be heard from the baby. Jo had had a miscarriage. But on the 11th February 2007, Barry Button was born! Real joy this time. Alan spent many happy times with Barry sitting on his lap in the wheelchair. At first with someone holding onto Barry, to stop him from falling off, Alan was unable to hold him sufficiently. Of course, later, Barry would climb quite confidently onto his grandad's lap. We would all go along to the swimming baths in Bude, Alan and myself watching with pride at Barry's prowess in the water. Even from a few months old he was full of confidence, like a little fish, swimming along underwater. He had the lifeguards quite worried at the amount of time he would spend under water before re-surfacing. Today he represents his county at swimming. Alan idolised his first grandson. Someone that would carry the Button surname forward.

Lorna had now moved up country. This involved moving to other equine college nr Northampton and using her extensive knowledge to set up other equine courses. Including having research papers published. But the lure of home proved too much and she returned home, with her new partner.

Then started a fully comprehensive research programme into breeding. Her mare Sienna, who had competed up to intermediate level horse trial was put to the stallion Kuwait Beach. He had sired several prolific event horses, including Olympic silver medallist, Sleep Late. The first born was Sands of Time, aka Horace, a lovely, stand 4 square in the box colt. At 3 his training for the eventing scene began. He was going extremely well. Then one day at a training yard, he was exuberantly on his toes. The owner of the yard suggested bring out an old timer to settle him. Wow, he just exploded and sent Lorna hurling off into the distance. As she landed, she was in great pain from her shoulder. The ambulance was called and she was sent to Derriford Hospital, Plymouth. There they did all the tests, including an X-ray. Was it another broken neck in the family? No, all clear. The doc was writing up her discharge papers, when she went into a deep sleep. Good, I thought, that is OK just resting. When she awoke though - good grief, all the signs of a stroke, dropped mouth and slurred speech. I rushed to the nurse station; alarm bells started. I sat worrying by her bed and at long last her partner arrived. I told him it might be brain damage. He nearly fainted. I was to leave her with him. It had been 7 hours since I had been home to talk to Alan. I got a taxi from Plymouth to home and reported back my time with his dear daughter at the hospital. Later that evening she arrived home after being discharged. We were rather surprised to say the least! The next day Nick was to come over to say Lorna was not at all well. She had collapsed.... I phoned for an ambulance and went with her. She started fitting violently in the ambulance. The paramedic said "if that was my daughter, I would be worried." She was taken in A and E at Exeter this time and again she started fitting. The medical team was called and she was rushed into resus. Then a 'shooting' victim had arrived and they left Lorna to deal with this incident. After some time, I was told she could be left now and for me to go home.

She was discharged again next day, but obviously still not "right", so back to hospital again, where at long last she has a brain scan. This showed she had suffered a cervical artery dissection causing a clot on her left cerebellum; hence her balance was "knackered"! She was transferred back to Derriford in case neurosurgical intervention was needed. She spent several days there, then was again moved back to Exeter nearer home. When she got back to RDE the ward staff said "Hello you back again!" The day came for discharge and Alan and I went to pick her up. I went into Okehampton, where she had been living, to ask for some medical back up for someone who had just been discharged with a stroke. They refused, saying that she no was no longer living in their district. Lorna had moved back home a couple of weeks before and had not yet registered with our GP. I Contacted our GP and 2 nurses were sent out to see Lorna. I was completely in the dark as to her nursing needs............. OK I knew how to care for someone with a spinal injury, but not care of a person post stroke. I am NOT a drama queen, but drama seems to happen in our lives!!

I feel I must now go back to Alan and his struggles. The powers to be decided to close Winsford Hospital, our cottage hospital. This place had been such a haven for Alan and a dependable source of nurses to care for him. The nurses came to care for Alan at home and occasionally he would go to the cottage hospital for 'bed and breakfast'. This meant he could go there in the evening, be got to bed with all the necessary functions, and then got up again in the morning, have breakfast, then to be toileted, washed and dressed, and sent home to me for the day. It gave me a lovely 'night off'. I knew that Alan had complete confidence in the nursing staff there, so I was happy. Unfortunately, the authorities decided Winsford was costing too much to run and yet again budgets came into things. There was a public outcry from everyone. Meetings were held in the local village hall. One of the guys on the top table, ex RAF I believe, (what would he know about the needs of the local community?) told the audience what an unruly group they were! Everyone had been haranguing him. Another group of nurses from Winsford took a coach up to Downing St. with a petition. Alas, this was all to no avail. Now the NHS is crying out for remedies to solve the current bed blocking in major hospital. How short sighted was the decision to close Winsford?

After the closure of Winsford Alan had been assured by the health authorities that community nurses would visit to attend to Alan's needs. Of course, this didn't transpire. Alan was then able to get Direct Payments, whereby Alan's medical care was to be 50% free at the point of delivery. 50% social care needs, which Alan would have to pay for. A long, long battle ensued about this over the coming years. More on this a bit later in the section regarding meeting with the "authorities" at Exeter airport.

Alan was approaching his 60th birthday. For a surprise, Lorna, Gavin and our daughter-in-law had arranged for him to go on a helicopter trip. The weekend arrived. My son had got a new car. On Alan's arrival downstairs that morning, he was trying to have a peaceful cup of coffee. "Hurry up, Gavin wants to take you for a trip in his new car", "Oh OK!" So, we bundled him into the car and off we went. Jo decided she wanted to go and visit a beach she remembered from her childhood. Mr Grumpy, Alan, didn't really fancy a beach trip, sand in everything. Then we stopped. "Ahh" said Alan, "now we are lost!" Gavin started opening some double gates. "You don't need to open the gates to do a 3-point turn!" grumbled Alan. But as we drove through the gates, lo and behold there was a helicopter. Good grief Alan thought, now realising what was in store, how am I going to get into that? Several strong men later and Alan was on board. The pilot took us up to North Devon, then back to our house, where Lorna had written a message in her sand school, "HAPPY BIRTHDAY DAD", then over Dartmoor to the Plymouth dockyards and coastline. Coming back, my son asked about some foolhardy manoeuvre about "dropping" - auto rotation, which the pilot then proceeded to show us. Skimming along the hedgerows, "anyone want to pick some blackberries?" He so loved that trip and would reminisce so often to his friends. Such a lovely surprise for him.

BACK TO AUTHORITIES

Another 'mad idea from the government 'Fairer Charging scheme'. A person from the Citizens Advice Bureau, employed by the authorities came to assess Alan's needs. We said "I thought the CAB was on the Citizens side, not to be employed by the government." "Ah well" she said, "If you should tell me any untruths, I cannot report these back". What a nonsense! Anyway, her findings were, that nearly all of Alan's benefits would be seized, leaving him with only £50 a week to live on and support his wife! Ludicrous!! So, another cry to the Spinal Injuries Association, for support. They gave us a detailed list of all the special disabled living finances needed for a person living with a spinal cord injury. Extra heating, laundry for the incontinence, wear and tear on the doors skirting boards etc, from wheelchair damage. The list was endless. It was astonishing when you sat down and thought about it, all the extras needed from a life in a wheelchair. Shortly after the government scrapped that idea, but we had yet again more stressful times and meetings.

So back to Direct Payments. This was a benefit that would allow Alan to have the monies from the authorities to arrange and pay for his own care, instead of being allotted carers that THEY thought would be proficient to care for Alan with his complex needs. We were asked to go to a meeting at the hospital. Those present were a senior district nurse and some social workers but NOT his doctor. I thought this was unfair so asked for an independent assessor to see Alan and his spinal care needs. This doctor duly turned up. This was when I asked, if she was a spinal cord specialist doctor, she said "no I deal with geriatric patients".

Alan was about 50 at that time. So again, much annoyance. Again, at yet another meeting, we were introduced to a Ms. Brown., who was going to assess Alans needs. She admitted to us that she had no knowledge of Spinal Injuries. Her previous role had been with people with learning difficulties. Another tear hair out time!

The outcome of all these meetings was to determine that Alan's care needs were 50% medical and 50% social. Alan would have to pay for the social care needs. Several years of battling this decision prevailed. Alan was trying to argue the point that ALL of his needs were due to a medical need. Very high cervical cord injury – not merely a "broken neck"! And most certainly NOT old age. An unfortunate mistaken phrase at the time was 'diselderly' - joining up of two descriptions disable and elderly. Alan was 50 at this time.

One of these meeting was held in Exeter. A large building opposite Exeter Airport. No, unfortunately we were not flying off on an exotic holiday. Just fighting for Alan's rights. We were ushered into a small room to wait. We were kept waiting quite a long time. A person came to apologise for keeping us waiting, "Is there anything I can get you?" "A large G&T" I said – Mmmm! Anyway eventually, we sat round a table, facing a panel of 'experts'.

Again, going through all the elements of Alan's care. We seemed to be going round in circles. Alan then dropped the bombshell. "Well, when I appeared in the high court in London to claim damages from my ex-employer for negligence, the then Harrow Health Authority was called for the defence. This person was to say "The health authority would be liable for all Alans care for life", thus depleting the amount of quantum – SORTED!

It was very difficult to find suitable carers. Long gone were the days when we would have the district nurses arriving. I would place adverts all around in local shops. I once asked if I could place an advert on the hospital notice board. Oh No, I was told. - "Well, you look after him!" I felt like saying!

One night the booked carer did not turn up. These are the days now, due to ageing I could no longer do the standing transfer lift. No carer. Phoned her home no answer. Phoned more people on the books, nobody was available. So, nothing else for it. Got the bedding from upstairs. Tipped Alans wheelchair back. Fortunately, it was a very versatile chair that could go back and legs up, so into a sort of reclined chair position. Tucked him up in the bedding and left him in his study for the night. Left the walkie talkie to hand and the heater on and went to bed. Next morning Cynthia arrived, quite oblivious as to where Alan had spent the night. Full of apologises, but again another hurdle. Another time we were snowed in and the carer of the time, Diane Smale, arranged for her son to bring her down in his tractor. We were both so grateful. Going above and beyond. Thank you, Diane!

OUTSIDE INTERFERENCE.

Instead of using the tried and tested cervical stand lift, those who should be obeyed insisted that Alan used a piece of lifting equipment. This involved placing a strap around his back whilst he was sat in the wheelchair and electrically getting him into a standing position passively. But as this did not allow Alan to engage his stomach muscles during the standing procedure, upon becoming upright he would lose consciousness due to the drop in blood pressure caused by this passive action.

This was the main difficulty in all of the years Alan was crippled. Some carers would turn up, reckoning they knew all about how to care for Alan. One telling me I needed to support his head whilst he was lying across the bed to put lower half clothing on – utter rubbish and totally impractical! If I'm supporting his head, how can I be at the other end taking his clothes off??!! Senior district nurse telling

Alan he did not need to be on the toilet for nearly an hour for a bowel evacuation. Well, you come back later in the day and try to get trousers and pants off after an explosion! She was NOT his full-time carer and had no in-depth knowledge. Later we were to find a marvellous book published by the Spinal Cord Injuries Association called Bowel and Bladder management. This was in black and white 'do not let your bowel evacuation be rushed' an hour is quite normal. This nurse was later to appear in court re her daughter's ill treatment of her grandchild!!

Then a Mr. Simcock from Health and Safety came to assess Alan. He said Alan needed two people to manoeuvre him. Come off it! They couldn't at times find one! I asked Mr. Simcox how was I to manage, when so many times I was the sole carer. He was non-committal. His idea was a non-starter. Two people arrived, one nearly 6' the other, barely 5'. They stood either side of Alan and heaved him to his feet, yanking his poor shoulder dreadfully, not using the tried and tested Cervical stand lift. This caused him much shoulder pain for several days. Another time, two carers were in the bathroom with him. I was cross because I had told them he would need a chair with the brakes on behind him at all times when he was stood, because if he was to spasm, which was feasible, he would crash to the ground. They had left him standing hanging onto a grab rail, he spasmed and went down. Fortunately, nothing broken this time. I do wish people would listen to me. I had been looking after him so long and knew of the dangers. One of the things that would annoy me when he was told he must have two carers (what nonsense that was) they would just chat between them over his head, as though he wasn't there. Then again, the powers to be changed their minds, and the 2-carer idea was scrapped - I think the phrase is FFS!!

Another time we were called to be evaluated for a new wheelchair, the latest lightweight model. Alan was quite impressed. I said that would help me so much in lifting his chair into the boot of the car. "Oh no, YOU are not here to be evaluated." Hard luck me then!

Alan had advertised in the local newsagent for care staff. This was to be via direct payments. Sue Brace turned up. We interviewed her and she seemed bubbly and competent. At all these interviews Alan would stress to the interviewees "this is the way my body works now, so this is the way I shall need to be looked after". So, after the interview, Alan and I both rushed out to get some shopping. It was whilst waiting for me to get the goods he started to be sick. I found an old carrier bag that he could be sick in. We hastened to get home. The vomiting continued until tea time. By now, his stomach was spewing up 'coffee granules' Time to call for an ambulance. Alan was to remain in hospital for 5 weeks. Every day for the 5 weeks the new carer drove both me and her into hospital for us to carry out a manual bowel evacuation. The sister in charge would not perform such a thing. I went to ask if I could pull the curtains round the bed and perform this. "Oh no" she said, I just ignored her and carried out the procedure. It could be fatal is this was not carried out. See notes Autonomic Dysreflexia. It proved that no hospital would carry out this evacuation. (Except of course a specialised SCI hospital) So every time Alan had to go into hospital, I and a carer would have to do this.

It turned out he had a condition known as hiatus volvulus. This reflux condition he would have to contend with until the end of his days. Sometimes it would disperse, but other times despite medication it would be another trip into hospital. The pain during these attacks was horrendous. It was to curtail any trips to restaurants. One time we had to leave hurriedly because he was starting to feel very sick. I used to keep plastic bags in the car in case of sickness. Even the stay in hospital for the hiatus volvulus was a long stay because he had developed pneumonia whilst waiting for the op. He was so poorly on one visit, that he just told me to go. I contacted Stoke Mandeville, THE SCI hospital and they liaised with Exeter hospital and suggested an antibiotic. On the next visit he was on the mend HURRAH. Sue, the new carer, had a wonderful sense of humour that came to the fore. One day I was performing the obligatory bowel evacuation and I said "your face is looking much better Alan.", (his face was very blotchy from a reaction to the hospital soap). Sue thought it was hilarious, because as I said this, I was looking at his bum!! I sometimes had to laugh or end up in tears.

Alan was to be discharged and the hospital had phoned the care agency that we were using at the time, to ask if she would have staff to send into Alan when he was home. Yes, all agreed. The day came and a phone call from Thelma, the agency owner, to say she didn't have any available carers. Obviously, we sacked this agency! In a panic I ran over to a neighbour, Kate, who was working locally as a carer. She immediately stepped into the breach. I had hired some electric heaters but when Kate and I plugged them in, they fused all the electrics. What a day! It was still a joy to have Alan home again.

So many ambulance calls:

Procedure: "Which service please?"

"Ambulance" - then a list of what I thought, banal questions. "Who is it for? What is the problem? Is he conscience? Can we speak to him?" Luckily, we had a cordless phone, three in fact. One in his study, one in the kitchen and one in his bedroom. Sometimes these questions from the call centre would seem to be taking for ever. Then, "We will send someone. Make sure any pets are shut away. If his condition worsens, please get back to us."

Once we were waiting for FIVE hours! At one stage I went outside to wait. I flagged down a passing van that looked like a medical vehicle, no it wasn't! The driver thought I was nuts. It was always such a relief to see a medic. They were always so calm and re-assuring. Doing lots of tests. Sometimes it would be a hospital trip. Others they had some magic potions in the bag and Alan would be able to sigh a relief as he was tucked up into bed and they were on their way. Always seem to be a 2-person team. One talkative and the other quiet. I will tell of the very last trip later when he would never see home again.

So many times, I fought to save Alan's life. Stoke had done a marvellous job in bringing him back to us. He had had many years of relatively 'good' health, but during the last few years of his life, health wasn't so good. The time when he was in hospital, waiting for a hiatus volvulus operation, he contracted pneumonia. Constant phone calls to Stoke and back to RDE Exeter, asking them to liaise with each other, with the specialist knowledge that the spinal unit had on a spinal cord injured person. I also yet again phoned the one and only Joyce saying please pray for him, "we already have" she replied. We saved the day between us, my worrying, Joyce's prayers and the hospitals.

Again, in N. Devon hospital, when he had to be intubated (negligence), I wasn't going to keep quiet. A complaint procedure was initiated.

I shall mention here, of previous stays and the routine. After the admission, telephone calls to the hospital. "What ward was he now in?" Another call first thing in the morning before 8am to find out what sort of night he had had. Tell him I shall be up later. Perhaps to get a message to me if there was anything he needed. This was depending on how ill he was. Then later in the day to speak to a doctor if possible. All of these visits would be curtesy of the carer on duty for that day. I had no transport, and it would be part of their work day.

The long stay in N DEVON hospital was punctuated by humour. After he had recovered somewhat, we all became aware of the chap in the bed by the door. He had a loud booming voice. Asking his son in a true Devon accent "bring me some of that pie. You know what I like, coronation pie!" What he meant was gala pie! For some reason the carer found it very amusing. The whole ward would get to know of his love for gala pie! Another time in the lift with the same carer I said of the lift voice, this chap must get fed up telling people what floor we were at. He replied "he has his up and downs." Thank goodness for a sense of humour in the stress times.

NEW NEIGHBOURS (2)

In 1995, much to our amazement, the agricultural field adjoining our property was given planning permission to build a local needs house. The building went ahead. Even though we objected most strongly. It was after all a green field site in open countryside! Throughout the build, I had numerous callers asking where the new house was. As I said it was on a field, not within sight of our lane. Therefore, nobody had any idea a house was going up there. We did, because it was to the east of our boundary, our house faced south. I asked the new owners if could they put a sign up with directions to their new house, this was not forthcoming. So, I had to get a bit of wood and paint a sign and put it onto the field gate post. What annoyed me the most was after the newcomers had moved in, one night I was putting Alan into bed, and yet again the backdoor bell rang. I had got Alan lying across the bed, taking his shoes and socks off. I had to leave him and go down. Saw somebody yet again asking directions. I was so cross I just ignored him and went back to where I had left Alan getting cold. The amazing thing was the next day, this new neighbour came to the door and called me all the names under the sun because I wouldn't open the door to HER caller. It had made me so cross about the non-realisation of dealing with someone such as Alan. But I suppose you have got to 'have been there' to get any idea.

Our next project was to create a lake. Our field at the bottom of the valley was forever 'boggy' as all the fields around drained into this particular field and then into the river. The local farmer did not want to rent this particular field because it was so difficult getting tractors onto such a wet area. So, with no more ado we contacted Luke Furse, a local earthmoving and plant hire contractor. We both watched in great excitement as the diggers, dumpers and other ancillary vehicles turned up. They would work into the evening with the lights on their tractors. This was early February and amazingly the rain fall was nil, so work went ahead uninterrupted. It was taking marvellous shape with an island in the middle. Alan, being the adventurer, wanted to drive down, in his car, into the base of the lake. We were towed in by one of the dozers and had a breath-taking sight of the lake to be, in its empty state, almost like sitting in a bomb crater. We were then towed back out again by the dozer. Luke was desperately hoping the tow rope wouldn't break! The only downside was the brakes had become covered in mud. We had to drive very gingerly into the car wash. "Where on earth have you been?", said an astonished operator. We then had to get the car taken back to Adaptacar to get the brakes sorted. The car wash had been overwhelmed….

The lake turned into a lovely haven for wildlife, Canadian geese being consistently the main residents. Other ducks and waterfowl also arrived. One day sitting down there with the dogs, I had the pleasure of the company of a kingfisher. The heron would become most disgruntled at times when we visited, interrupting his fishing time. Of course, we had to get a boat for our lake. Sadly, Alan would say" You know I shall never be able to use it"

FRUSTRATIONS OF COPING WITH NHS AND SOCIAL ORGANISATIONS

There was to follow numerous meeting with authorities. Alan in the meantime was hiring his own carers and still contributing financially to his 'social care' needs, despite the original High Court ruling stating that "The health authority would be liable for all Alans care for life".

At one point the NHS part was to be supplied by NHS staff and then the social by local authority staff. This caused problems in as much that NHS staff would arrive to do MBE. Then leave, and Alan would be sat shivering whilst social care staff would arrive to get him into the shower. This could mean a wait of between 30 - 60 minutes! The kind hearted nurses from Winsford were not prepared to go along with this malarkey, so, they undertook the whole routine!

Then was to come Continuing Health Care. This would put Alans care back in the hands of authorities with them deciding who would come in to be his carers and to decide on what sort of care he needed. As part of this "need determination", they decided that his bowel evacuation should be observed by, wait for, it a team of SIX people! They would all be crowded into his bathroom/ bedroom to watch the process. Can you imagine of a more demeaning experience for the poor man? Having to have a shit with 6 people watching!! They then could not find a suitable agency to take on Alan's complex care needs. Alan had been having these complex care needs met for the last 30plus years, predominantly by me. But no, this time the authorities came up with 'THEIR' solution. Alan would have to go into a care home! NO- we did not think so!!

The authorities could not find a suitable home care package, thereby not fulfilling their duty of care. They were set on transferring him into a very small room in a care home on an Industrial estate! The room would not have been adequate for Alan's large wheelchair - for turning, the necessary space in the toilet area for Alan and the carer to perform the bowel evacuations. They couldn't attend to the necessary bowel evacuations in a hospital, so goodness knows how he would have fared, miles away from me and our lovely countryside home, with untrained staff. It was NOT my idea he went into a home. They could not fulfil their duty. A new doctor arrived at our house, patted Alan on the shoulder and said "best place for you in a home"!! I hit the roof and said to him "you have just signed his death warrant!" I had loyally cared for him for the past forty years.

Alan contacted the local BBC Spotlight TV news. They sent the health correspondent and her team round to see us at home. They spent all day filming Alan in his home environment, with his carer. The day went very well and we had a huge response the next day. Spotlight had featured Alan's story on the early morning news, lunch time, afternoon, tea time and late evening. The response was overwhelming and we had such a lot of calls, expressing their sympathy for Alan's plight.

We would often say "We make a good team both of us", just fighting to keep him at home and safe.

We had seen an advert in the Spinal Injuries Newsletter for Active Assistance. We suggested this agency to the powers to be. Low and behold we were allowed to employ Active Assistance. I

remember saying to Alan. Good if anything should happen to me you would be cared for.
Unfortunately, this proved not to be a happy time. I had to oversee the giving of all his medications, creams etc. and to show them how to take blood pressure. They were to live in 24/7 and the majority would be from Eastern Europe, some with very little knowledge of English. So poor Alan did not only have to explain his bodily functions but also contend with and try to overcome the language barrier. They would stay approximately a fortnight, and then another person would turn up and the whole process to be repeated by poor Alan. From my point of view, they were not the cleanest of people to have living in your home. Also, the number of breakages and stealing was growing alarmingly. I think I was the one to say "NO, enough is enough" and we were left to find our own agency. This was via a local agency. It surprised both Alan and myself that we had to go to the agency in Okehampton, and be 'interviewed' by the manager and the carers. This was not the way we did things. We were the ones to do the interviewing at our home, of potential cares. We needed carers, so on we go again. But they would have control who they sent into Alan. Not always a good choice. One day I remember trying to get a bit of 'me' time, and hiding in my bedroom and shutting the door. Male carer

came in, no knocking, "Oh there you are". At one stage one of the carers was drunk on duty. When Alan reported this. The manager took umbridge and said she would remove the whole team of three. Again, left in the lurch through no fault of Alan's. I had to take on Alan's care full time again, with help from Lorna doing the handling. Alan made contact with the Continuing Health Care authority and told them it was a desperate situation. They agreed to leave the funding in Alan's hands and he was to have the power to choose the staff HE wanted. Also, to get up and go to bed at the times he wanted. I remember him saying one evening in summer "I don't want to go to bed in the daylight!"

THE FAILINGS OF A GENERAL HOSPITAL

The next disaster came. Alan's doctor had diagnosed a hernia, which would need an operation. Alan said the safest place for this to be carried out would be in a specialist spinal unit in Salisbury Hospital (known as Oddstock in the "trade"). This was duly undertaken, again, having a long stay. It was whilst at "Oddstock" his anaemia was to come to the fore and blood transfusions were needed. Eventually the op was undertaken and Alan was again with me at home. It was lovely to have him home again. But just a week later he got a UTI (urinary tract infection). He was admitted to North Devon hospital and put onto intravenous antibiotic fluids. I thought he was improving. Then one day I went to visit and he was gasping for air and slipping into unconsciousness. I rushed to the nurse's desk to ask what on earth was happening. We went back to his room. The anaesthesia chap was just going into Alan. By now the crash team had turned up. One of them turned to me and said "What is his quality of life like, is it worth intubating him? I was utterly dumbstruck. "Of course, it is why on earth not??!!", they asked me to leave the room. I refused and made myself very small in the corner. I watched in dismay as the metal tubes were passed down Alan's throat. I then went and waited in the corridor. Perhaps I should phone my son and tell him Dad might be dying. I only had the carer with me at the time. The nurse came out with Alan being wheeled on a trolley. Nobody told me what was going on. It seemed an eternity before any one came to speak to me. I imagined they were laying his body out and I would be asked to go and see him at any moment. But no, the nurse came to tell me that Alan was in intensive care and I could go to see him. By this time my son had arrived from Cheltenham. I just fell into his arms and cried with relief. Now my daughter had also arrived. I didn't feel so lonely and frightened. We all went down to see dad. He did look so ill. The staff in the unit were so gentle and caring. They advised we could go home but come back to visit any time day or night over the next 24 hours. He slowly recovered and was given a bed in the general ward until discharge. I had asked if he could be transferred to Salisbury Hospital Spinal Unit after this fiasco and having no confidence in the hospital. I was denied this request. I then opened a case against the hospital via PALS. It would seem that the doctor and staff had been negligent in Alan's care. The drip he was on wasn't being monitored correctly. Because of Alan's inability to breath normally due to the SCI, his lungs were just filling up and he was drowning. I tried to approach the doctor concerned to get some information on what caused Alan to end up in the Intensive Care Unit -was it a chest infection? He just said "No" and turned his back on me. Such arrogance. He had also told Alan, 'that was a close call'. I had avoided mentioning to Alan, that he had nearly died. During the next few weeks, after trying to get to the bottom of things, I was unable to ascertain what exactly had happened. PALS got involved and the medical report said: "fluid overload after treatment with fluids"

The trust and the doctor were to give me a very half-hearted apology, about what had happened to

Alan during his care from this doctor. We vowed NEVER to be at that hospital again!!

The story of Alans dreadful experience at N.D. Hospital was published in the Spinal Injuries Association. A newsletter dedicated to spinal cord damage.

Whilst waiting outside ICU at N.D. Hospital I met a chap I knew. We both looked at each, trying to think who we were in this place. Then it dawned, he was my electrician. The usual question 'how are you'. Of course, neither of us were. Alan had been rushed down from the ward, after being intubated. Darren was with his wife. Her mother was also in ICU.

TOWARDS THE END.

Alan physical abilities (and mine) had been in some decline over the past 10 years. "Time and Tide wait for no man." Despite all the determination Alan had put to the last 30 years, he was finding the effort more and more irksome. The standing ability had weakened, finding more and more difficulty in the effort of being heaved into a standing position. Even driving, which he had loved, became more laborious. At the end he had given up driving and the carers had to take over. Alan had to become a passenger. There were to be no more trips, with it being just Alan and myself. I was finding it difficult to come to terms with. Also of course so was Alan.

In the last couple of years of Alan's life, he would sweat profusely, to the extent he would need a towel on his lap during the day, that he could mop his brow with. You would think this was a precursor to an autonomic dysreflexia attack. But it did not develop into that. The doctors didn't seem able to come up with an answer.

We used to enjoy completing the Choice magazine crossword every month. By the time I got round to having a look Alan had completed it. He has such an active and intelligent brain.

The doctors had been trying to correct his anaemia for several years without success. There should have been alarm bells ringing when he had to have the hernia operation. Before they could perform the operation, he had to have a blood transfusion. No mention was made as to why this was. He seemed to take a long time to pick up after this latest hospital treatment.

Then in December 2013, he was diagnosed with Leukaemia. I had gone shopping with one of the carers. It was coming up to Christmas. Lorna was at home with her dad doing the carers payroll and rotas, when the doctor turned up to tell Alan the devasting news. The carer and I had arrived back with Christmas things, quite joyful. I found Lorna in tears in Dad's study. "What, what??" I asked. She told me the ghastly news. I rushed upstairs to Alan. He had been spending days in bed sometimes. "We must talk Jan", he said in such a sad voice. I think my first question after he told me his news was "So what is the treatment?" Nobody seemed to know. We were all in shock, including the carer who had been waiting downstairs with Lorna.

The next day the doctor had arranged for Alan to go into hospital for tests. We all, Lorna was with us, went into the consultant's office. He told Alan he was going to take a sample from Alan's sternum. He said it would be very painful, similar to the pain felt when having a heart attack. The test was undertaken. Lorna told me dad's face had gone ashen. I didn't see it. I must have been looking elsewhere and praying. Yes, the test confirmed, it was blood cancer. There are so very many different sorts of these cancers. I thought the consultant was a bit vague as to which one Alan had succumbed to.

That Christmas 2013 was a flashback to 1969, when he had recently broken his neck. Everyone round his bedside for the celebrations. This year we all spent time with him, but he was getting very tired, so we left him to sleep. This was to be his last Christmas.

The treatment apparently was blood transfusions. One every month. So be it I thought. If that is what will be needed, OK let's do it. We, I say we as Lorna had always come with us and also one of the carers to do the manoeuvring, went to the hospital for the transfusions. As the blood was going into Alan's vein, the change was remarkable. My old Alan was returning. His face lit up and the old smile was there. One weekend I spent the whole-time panicking, because I thought they had given him the wrong blood group. Nobody at the local hospital had any notes. On the Monday, I rang the hospital again and was told the blood group from the blood in the transfusion Alan had been given was 'a general purpose one' and anyone could have it. At this time also, Alan was getting pressure sores. Throughout all this time he had been completely free of them, except for the first night in the London Hospital, when he had one develop on his heel.

Stoke Mandeville soon cleared that up, but alas this time, they were proving difficult to heal.

This new routine continued for several months. One time on a visit to the Exeter hospital, we were to be told, "no transfusion needed". "Oh good", I thought, "he must be getting better". In hindsight, I realised the transfusions were futile. One of the carers had left, "rats leaving a sinking ship". Alan started to yet again advertise for new carer. He was spending more and more time in bed during the day. Now none of Alans' lovely smiles were happening. We did have a few interviews with potential carers, but I think they somehow found out of Alan's disease and prognosis. Then another carer wanted to take a holiday unexpectedly. She recommended a friend to cover her absence. He turned up to have some training with the other carer who had left. I must admit we weren't very impressed, but desperate times. Now Alan was also getting severe neck aches. Poor man, after all his struggles over the years.

Then Alan was admitted into hospital once again. He was in there for a week and then discharged home. There was some mumbled talk about sepsis. The carer who was away on 'holiday' had not returned, so the 'new carer was in attendance. I spent the next few days, constantly running up and down stairs to advise the new carer. He was obviously not as experienced as we were led to believe. The bowel evacuations were non-existent and the whole time Alan spent in bed. I managed to get him to eat and he was to have very basic care needs undertaken. At the end of that week, we once more went into hospital. Last trip. Again, ambulance personnel, I said I have done all the first aid I know, but to no avail. He told me I had done everything possible, but the situation needed more than I could give. So again, bundle into the lift with difficulty, and down into the ambulance. We both knew the routine so well. But this time my dear Alan was sinking. I was supposed to be strapped into a passenger seat, but throughout the whole journey, he kept asking if I was there, is it much farther, are we nearly there. The paramedic gave up asking me to sit down and 'buckle up' On arrival we were met by a nurse, whos' apron was covered in plaster. I said you been getting plastered? Weak joke. I then said to her "take care of him." She asked if he always this colour? Poor man was a yellow hue. I knew then I think this was to be the last trip into hospital. Lorna and I sat by his bed in A&E. he was delirious. Asking us to take his hat off, it wasn't even on.

The carer had come back from holiday. She went and 'cared' for his needs on the Monday. I had taken the day off. The next day Tuesday, the carer took me to visit and do a bowel evacuation. I was a bit late arriving and Alan was very agitated. "where have you been? I thought there must be an accident." This was all part and parcel of the disease taking hold. He had a bite to eat at lunch time. They were trying to arrange for the physiotherapist to come and put him on a nebuliser. But the nebuliser wasn't working. Then for the very first time in our lives, Alan shouted at me "get it off.". I was told that he had pneumonia. He whispered to the physios, "I did try". We were then to wait for the doctor to try and drain his chest. The time was now 4pm and I wandered down to get a cup of tea, we had been with him since 10.30am. On my return the thorax consultant had arrived. They had got him sitting on the edge of the bed, with the carer in attendance. The consultant said he would come back the next day and try again. Paul went to lie him back down but we all noticed that he had soiled himself. Paul was trying to clean it up. I said "No Paul, leave it, look at him". He was unconscious. I did say to the carer Paul, in desperation, try to wake him up. Paul had a large booming voice. "Alan!" he shouted. Alan's eyes flashed open, but immediately closed again. Sigh….

The next thing I remember was the curtains being pulled round and a young female doctor, taking me outside. I was to be told death is imminent. I still could not believe that what she was saying was going to be true. I said to Paul, will you go back and collect Lorna. I didn't want her to hear from me on the phone "your father is dying". It would be a 2-hour round journey before Paul would be back with my daughter. My first thought was to phone dear Joyce. She had been with me at the very start of these troubles. I went back to his bedside and sat on the chair holding his hand. He was in a coma. Lorna arrived at 6pm, to see the curtains pulled round the bed.

A drunken prisoner was put into the bed opposite. He was kicking off in a dreadful manner with 2 guards sat by his bed. At this stage Alan was unconscious, but Paul the carer went and had a word – saying this is not acceptable. They then moved Alan down the corridor into a private room.

We then continued to sit by his bed, chattering on. I do believe he could hear me. He had said, that when one time he had become unconscious in the 'lifting equipment' he could still hear us calling him.

At one stage his arm came out, as if he wanted to cuddle us. We sat like this for hours. Paul had gone off somewhere. It got to 11 o'clock at night. Paul had been on duty since 9.30 that morning. I suddenly realised he wanted to get home. We made the decision to leave. "Cheerio Alan, we'll see you in the morning", The sister on duty said, "shall I phone you?". The phone rang at 4am May 22nd 2014 – 5 months after the leukaemia diagnosis.

I have wondered recently; I wish face book was around then. I could have opened a page for him and shared the times he spent in hospital with his other friends, in the outside world. I think that would have been lovely.

More about the funeral. The only attendees were Bern and Pauline (friends who had known Alan for longer than I had), Gavin and his wife and Lorna and her partner. I remember going along the dual carriageway and we passed a peculiar estate car. We all thought "what is that funny vehicle? Its rather unusual", then realised it was dear Alan's very last trip into Exeter. At the crematorium, I sat surround by my children and their partners, pretty well oblivious to the happenings. I had chosen the song Bring in the Clowns. There is one line was so apt to us both. "one who keeps tearing around, one who can't move" Lorna and her father had a joint love of the Rolling Stones, so she had chosen Sympathy for the Devil, which they both used to enjoy. Plus, the wonderful Queen song "These are the days of our lives".

The ceremony over, we all went to a very nice country pub. Although I had to have my say to people about a dog they had left shut up in their car. Nothing changes. The next few weeks continued unnoticed, by me. I do wish that people realised I was so overcome with grief I couldn't talk to anyone. Please forgive me now. Wonderful solicitations on all the bereavement cards. No one ever had a bad word to say about my beloved.

"Those days are all gone now."

Stand up now Alan and walk into the next life…….

Despite all the atrocities he had to suffer. Alan retained his dignity until the last.

Goodbye my beloved…….

"Out of suffering have emerged the strongest souls. The most massive characters are seared with scars "

Khali Gibran

I am now going to add some excerpt from my diaries for the years 2012 & 2013, the last two years of my beloved man's life. Illustrating the problems finding suitable carers, and the wherewithal to pay for such care

Active Assistance. (mainly eastern European personal assistants)

January 2012- PA told me the pillow was dirty and I needed to wash it. This was despite my giving the Pas clean sheets pillowcases and duvet covers at every 'change over' some would not even bother to put fresh bedding on. Preferring to sleep on a bare mattress and pillow.

Jack new carer – very poor understanding of English, asking me for a basket. He actually meant bucket.

31st Jan. started enquires about another Oswestry standing frame.

2013.

8th February went to meeting about receiving direct payments

13th February no news from PCT (Primary care trust)

Zara worked from 8th thru until 11th then quit. Alan did have very complex care needs.

14th February PCT told Alan he must have "pinny girls" or go into home, they being unable to find suitable qualified staff. Please, let Alan have the funds and he will train people to his standards. So, we had to continue with AA.

21st April new PA broke slow cooker. Knob came off in her hand. Not repairable. Lorna had recently bought this for me as a Christmas present.

8th July another PA – how careless. Alan slid of shower chair. Nothing broken.

25th Justin another PA so arrogant, and selfish. (this is not your home)

Justin would spend all evening cooking his meal. Master chief he is not. Using many various utensils and mess everywhere. I was tired and wanted to relax, but the noise emitting from the kitchen was alarming.

Justin told Alan he must not have heating in the bathroom because he was too hot. Poor Alan obviously naked having a shower, and his spinal condition necessitating the warmth.

29th Alan told Justin to go. Justin insisted that I should run him up to the bus stop. Why couldn't he walk?

Carlos arrived later that evening. English almost non-existent.

Broke lever in shower. Another plumber callout. Already the kitchen tap hose had been broken.

2May Marcin arrived back. The most excellent carer. Polish, but his English was as good as, if not better than mine.

15th May letter from PCT saying we must have AA for at least another 3 months. Still not doing their job. Alan in the meantime had asked me to place adverts for carers in all the local shops.

22nd May a Zimbabwean carer. English OK but would start cooking and frying meat at 11 pm!!

23rd May Alan not feeling too good.

28th Alan into Odd stock Spinal unit hospital. will need a hernia operation.

1st June visited Alan at Salisbury hospital.

3rd June Operation cancelled.

7th June Operation – 4 hours but needed blood transfusion. (looking back the alarm bells should have started then. Why a blood transfusion?)

10th June Alan home. So glad to see him

11th June Alan in bed all day.

12th 13th 14th still in bed. Visit from Doctor. Wound healing well.

15th up, but early to bed.

Alan is now saying he would like a ceiling hoist fitted. Up until now he had always managed a standing transfer into a shower chair and then into the bathroom. Is this just old age or is it something more sinister.?

Social service engineer told Alan a ceiling hoist could not be fitted on the ceiling, because it was a Lath and plaster ceiling. What tosh. Alan decided to get a loan and buy one privately. Arjo engineer came out to assess. No problems.

9th JULY ALAN CAN START RECRUITING FOR HIS OWN CARERS!!

Ads placed

20th July interviews 2 good. One no show.

30th got team.

5th August Meeting here at home. Carol Greene Commission Manager, Complex Care Team. Agreed Continuing Health Care. The government first introduced this act in 2007.

Alan has been attending numerous meetings. On more than one occasion cancelled at the last moment. Apparently double-booked appointments by the health officials. There were to be health assessments, by 'experts' that Alan and I both realised, had not the first idea of the complexities of SCI. Such a palaver to meet the criteria for CHC. This is an amount of money agreed by the government to allow people such as Alan, to pay for their own care. The criteria being a health need, and NOT social care. As Alan had been assed previously, for the health i.e., bowel management, then another amount for the 'social' need, washing etc. The health need being from NHS therefore 'free at the point of delivery' Social need, we had to pay for. For goodness sake, Alan has a broken neck what is there not to agree that this is a medical need. So, six years after this new act came into force, Alan has been awarded Continuing Health Care. Throughout all these preambles we had no useful support from any case worker. Alan carried out all the research himself. The amount of money wasted on arriving at this decision is unbelievable i.e., letters meeting etc etc.

7th Aug Kelsey started. Back in the old days when Alan was receiving direct payments, Kelsey's mother Sue was employed by Alan. Kelsey appears to be as good as her mum as a carer.

Lorna an ex-nurse also joined the team. Then Paul – no experience but cared for his father for some years. He was also willing to listen and learn. - so, our team of three.

8th Aug. visit from occupational therapist. No idea on how to handle a SCI person.

9th Aug. Farah leaves. This is the last of the Active Assistant staff.

10th Aug. My Lorna training Paul.

14th Kelsey being trained. Alan another UTI

25th August Lorna, my daughter agrees to take on the role of organising the rotas, payees, HMRC Etc. She is in the study going through procedures with Alan

1st September Alan poorly again. Docs are trying to boost his blood iron

18th Sept. Lorna (ex nurse) leaves. She is not prepared to do MBE.

My Lorna does evening shift.

22nd Sept. Lorna puts dad to bed, at 4.30. so tired of the carer's fiasco.

2ns October. I have shingles.

24th Nov. Alan has yet another UTI. Only once during the last 40years of his disability has Alan had a UTI. That was just after being discharged from Stoke Mandeville. Now they are very numerous. Alarm bells are starting to ring.

11 Dec. Doctor visits. Alan is diagnosed with leukaemia.

No more entries for this year.

2014

3 Jan. what a lovely surprise Bern and Pauline visit.

14th Jan Nurse to take bloods.

16th Blood transfusion Holsworthy hospital

22 New wheelchair cushions. To try to alleviate the pressure sores.

1st Feb. Letter from dog warden. It has been alleged that our dogs are straying and fouling the highway. (at the time we were having a herd of 50 milking cows back and forth past our house, and the accompanying mess!) Alan at this time was upstairs dying from cancer. He never got to see this letter.

2nd Feb. Alan still in bed – pressure sore and painful neck.

14th Feb still bad pressure sore. Alan had never before had a pressure sore in the last 40years plus of

his disability.

17th Feb Paul away (family crisis) Kelsey stepped.

26th Feb. up to Odd stock.

28th into Royal Devon and Exeter hospital.

7th March Buying loads of 'nibbles. Trying to counteract Alan's weight loss.

13th March Another blood transfer at hospital

23rd March Take on 2 extra carers for the night shift. I had been attending during the night. But getting no sleep.

27th March Doctor admitted Alan to hospital.

28th until 4th April carers attending Alan in hospital to carry out MBE

23rd April more advertisements for carers placed. Sue had left.

25th Interviewed Shelly and Ashley. Ashley comes recommended

11thMay employed Ashely – Paul training.

13th Kelsey unexpected away. Paul and Ashley.

14th Paul away. Just down to Ashely

17th Paul back.

19th Alan into RDE.

No more entries. As I am writing these entries from the diaries at the time, I am reliving the nightmare unfolding before us.

A WORD FROM THE MAN HIMSELF (a letter to friends)

Date- One hell of a long time since Stoke Mandeville.

My Dear Gail and Frans,
                    THE PROLOGUE

Since the arrival of your first "newsy" e-mail it was decided by "she who must be obeyed" that it was about time that I put pen to paper (metaphorically). I had been working on a reply for some time when your second e-mail arrived. Don't rush me! Don't rush me!

So here we go.

I've just been looking back through the letters on my computer and either I have never written to you (false) or I have never written to you since the introduction of Personal computers (true). This gives a contact ratio of ?:2. Some kind of friend or what?

When I posted the card at Christmas, I really thought we had lost contact. Thank God for modern technology! Anyway, with any luck you might get a copy of this round about January 2001. Question. Does anything ever change down here? Let's see!

I really can't remember at what stage the news of our mundane little lives had reached the last time I contacted you, so I'll do a Stephen Hawkin and give you a "brief history of time". It will probably be just as unintelligible as that book as well. Not that I have read it you understand!

LIFE AND STUFF

I shall now introduce you to a number of people who you don't know and probably will never meet, but who are instrumental to the continuing Button saga.

Trevor and Mavis Box, our long-term neighbours who farmed Rectory Farm, the property opposite, became tired of servicing a mortgage at the age of fifty plus and decided to sell-up. He put the farm on the market but retained an area of land adjoining us (Canna Park) for part time farming.

Trevor sold the farm to a Mr. and Mrs. Scumbag. (No that's not their real name). I shall gloss over the next period. Suffice to say they turned out to be neighbours from hell. We found it impossible to establish any kind of rapport with them. The relationship ended in litigation which we won. End of story. Scumbag died. Mrs. Scumbag put the farm on the market.

We put in an offer but Charlotte and Stuart Polhill topped our offer for Rectory Farm and moved down from Sussex, with their 4 teen-age children.

Trevor Box now sold Canna Park-the fields adjacent to us (you remember he retained these when he sold Rectory Farm to scumbag). Trevor and Mavis moved into Holsworthy (our nearest town of any size) and, much to our surprise, apparently love town life.

Richard Wooldridge a local farmer bought the whole sixty-five acre Canna Park at auction for a knock down price and I have been regretting ever since not having the bottle to top his offer.

Is this the story of my life or what? I used to be indecisive but now I'm not quite so sure.

Richard sold the field immediately over the hedge from us to a Paul Saunders. Paul incidentally was also unsuccessful at buying Rectory Farm, having sold his own house with that in mind he was now up shi.. a muddy creek. Paul has now built a house on that field. Astonishingly getting planning permission on what was a farmer's field. Strings were pulled.

You may gather that I am not to chuffed about the idea since I don't want any diminution of my splendid isolation. Or am I just a miserable old git jealous of anybody showing a bit of initiative? Moi? Naaah! Talking of miserable young git, what a laugh a minute Paul is. Not! Best keep my distance, I think.

Let us proceed. Are you still with me? Keep up. Keep up.

DELUDED?

Stuart Polhill decided to sell the fields below our house (formerly owned by scum bag and formerly - formerly by Trevor). In all about fourteen acres. So, having learned the lesson of what can happen when matters are taken out of one's control, I decided to try and buy the three fields. Turned out to be not too traumatic since it was only me and the before mentioned Richard bidding at the auction. Seems like he has grander ideas than me and deeper pockets. However, I was successful.

Thought. Paranoia – Definition - one suffering from delusions of grandeur-usually associated with the landed gentry.

So now we have some more problems to worry about. Hedging, ditching, draining, fencing soil analysis and shi… fertiliser application to mention but a few.

It was all going to work out well. Since Lorna was looking to expand her livery business to include fitness training, I could see an all-weather exercise track advancing up the fields –visions of Henry Cecil, Robert Sangster and Sheikh Mohamed of horse racing fame-and this time next year Rodney we'll be millionaires.

Then Lorna decided to get herself a proper job and moved to Sparsholt College in Hampshire as yard manager/instructor - more about that in a while.

BACK IN THE STICKS

Back in Devon. I started to get the estate (snigger snigger) back into shape. What a crap farmer scumbag was. It needed new hedge laying, banking with tracked digger (wonderful to watch these guys with their Tonka toys) there's still more to do, new fencing - an ongoing job, some drainage - more to do yet and new gates. All this to impress the farming neighbours or at least not be giggled at by them.

Then Stuart came over, almost in tears, to say he had been sacked from his job as area manager with Marks and Spencer. He had been virtually king of Cornwall. This after thirty years with the company and entertaining the chairman and his whole family when they rented a property on the Roseland peninsular in Cornwall for the summer. I have not been privy to the reasoning but he must have blotted his copybook in a big way because it was instant dismissal. The only explanation Stuart would volunteer was that he had "made an error of judgement that resulted in no pecuniary advantage to himself ".

I presume as a result of his reduced circumstances he decided to sell more of Rectory Farm land. This time another local farmer (the James') whose land also adjoins ours bought the seventeen acres that was up for grabs. They then started a program of reinstating the land including ploughing and reseeding. Since their latest purchase was not immediately available to them David James approached us to see if he could rent the Isted estate. So now the fields earmarked for loss making horses are at least producing an income. I guess it's an ill wind that blows nobody any good.

Where shall we go now? I know let's go to Cheltenham. Remember I still have a son? Gavin. He's now 33. I sometimes forget it myself.

BATHING IN REFLECTED GLORY?

When Gavin left school, he eventually got an apprenticeship at HM Dockyard in Plymouth. He finished his apprenticeship in the nuclear submarine re-fitting depot and then decided to pack it in and become a mature student. I must admit to being quite pleased at this news as I imagined him coming home and glowing in the dark. Nuclear-phobia or what.!

He left Plymouth University with a degree in Computing and Informatics and found himself a job as a programmer/systems analyst with the Marlborough Stirling Group based in Cheltenham. They produce software for banks and building societies. He arranged to rent a flat - right in the middle of town and only two minutes from the office.

We hired a box trailer packed his gear and moved him up over a weekend. It was a nice flat and convenient for all that the town offers. And what a nice place Cheltenham is. He hadn't been there very long when a house came on the market. Gavin made an offer and bought it. I was very impressed. It's a modern two-bedroom town house built on three floors with integral garage so he can park off street. There is a drawback of course; being on three floors the access is difficult for me. Who said well - planned Gavin? However, when we visit, we stay quite close, using our caravan, the site is only three miles from Gavin's house.

Last November Gavin decided, after talking to colleagues at MSG, to become self-employed. He set up a company, and now commutes to Bristol every day from Cheltenham. The Bristol and West Building Society outsource their computer programming to a company called Salmon something-or-other and he freelances for them at a squillion pounds an hour. So far it appears to be a good move and I think he's quietly pleased.

Although we don't see a great deal of him, we do keep in touch by telephone and e-mail (I'm becoming quite a techno-nerd in my old age). But then I don't think you could pay him enough to move back down this way. He has become a city dweller and considers Halwill to be cabbage land. Who can blame him?

He does appear to have a very active social life. When he was on the third year of his degree he was placed with Nuclear Electric at Gloucester. They had a very good sports and social club, which Gavin made full use of. He has kept in touch with old students and colleagues from NE and has quite a wide circle of friends. Gloucester is only a stone's throw from Cheltenham.

Last Autumn he went to Barbados for a holiday. Looked wonderful from the photographs and in March is off to Canada to try his hand (?) at skiing.

We were all together at Christmas for a family reunion and met Gavin's girlfriend Jo for the first time. Nice girl, not at all difficult to get on with, we are pleased for him. Probably too early to think of wedding bells yet. We were all invited to Lorna's for Christmas Day tea. A good time was had by all. Since that brings Gavin's news up to date where shall we go now?

How about picking up Lorna's story.

MOVING ON OUT

Lorna is now 28 and has had some considerable success with her equestrian competition career after leaving university with a degree in Chemistry and Biology. She enjoys Dressage and Show-jumping but her main interest is Horse Trials (Eventing). To fund her horsing stuff, she set up a livery yard. Just after we bought the extra land, Lorna decided her livery yard wasn't making enough money to support her equestrian competition career. Entry fees and transport were becoming more and more expensive. So, she looked around for a job that might provide better finance and include her interest in horses. Sparsholt Agricultural College in Hampshire was expanding their Equestrian unit so Lorna applied for and got the job as Yard Manager/Instructor.

She was able to take her horses with her on the basis that the students would be allowed to ride them. A three bed-roomed house was provided which she shared with another teacher. She worked such long hours however that there was not a lot of time for competition.

She saw an advertisement in the Horse and Hound magazine for a Lecturer at Moulton Agricultural

College in Northampton. Applied and was successful. This job allowed her to use her degree in Chemistry and Biology as well as her knowledge of horses. It should also have allowed her to continue competing-at least that was the theory. Lorna rented a house in Moulton and her partner; Nick found a job on a large civil engineering project in Birmingham which was within travelling distance.

What happened next? Oh yes, after Lorna left for Sparsholt our outbuilding, originally the coach house to the Rectory, started to deteriorate. She would knock the odd nail in here and there, which kept it in shape.

I decided to invest in converting it into a dwelling, which would allow us several options. Option one. We could let the whole kit and caboodle out to some crazy horse owning person looking for somewhere to set up a training yard.
Option two. We could let out just the coach house as a permanent let.
Option three. We could do summer holiday letting. Option four, which is not really an option, is to do up the coach house move in and sell Isted House.

We elected to go for option one - got planning permission and went ahead. I am quite pleased with the result. It's a two-bedroom cottage with entrance lobby, living/dining room, kitchen, bathroom, downstairs toilet, oil-fired central heating and double-glazing.

Having converted the coach house, we missed the storage space it had provided. So, I had a steel-framed barn built by Lorna's training arena. The arena occupies the old orchard and the barn now obscures the afore mentioned Paul's house.

I am destined not to become a millionaire. All those people, (mostly letting agents), who when we talked to them about the project, started drooling and getting dollar signs in their eyes, couldn't come up with the goods. Or at least come up with a decent tenant willing pay a reasonable rent. Who said we live in the sticks?

THE MOVING FINGER WRITES…

Fate stepped in at the right moment, or as it turned out stuck the boot in at the wrong moment. Shortly after Lorna moved to Northampton Tessa Counsel contacted her. Tessa is the head of the equestrian unit at The Duchy of Cornwall Agricultural College. That's about twelve miles from us. Tessa's husband is the principle. They were setting up a B.Sc. degree course at the college and needed academically qualified lecturers.

Whilst Lorna was at Moulton, she had been given the opportunity to take educational teaching qualifications which together with her degree allowed her to be well placed to be interested in Tessa's offer. Also, by this time she was coming to grips with the politics of the cloistered atmosphere of college life. In other words, watch your back. It was worse than a monastery, petty jealousy wise. Particularly since she had been co-author of a paper published in The Chemist journal about the early ancestry of the horse.

It appeared Tessa's proposal was just the vicar's knickers and at a most opportune time. So, Lorna handed in her notice to leave at the end of the academic year.

All she needed was a place to rent where she could live with Nick and her horses.
Dilemma or what? No contest really. Lorna came back to Devon with Nick and horses. She to take up Tessa's offer. He to find employment with local contractors. Both to live in the coach house.

Here is where the fate boot-sticking bit comes in. Unfortunately, the Duchy College couldn't get enough bums on seats. Consequently, they couldn't get funding for the course. The knock-on effect was that they could only offer Lorna a part-time lecturing position. Mean time Nick encountered a similar situation. Plenty of part-time work but of course only part-time pay.

RAYS OF SUNSHINE

It's not all doom and gloom however. Nick has gone back to Southampton. Commuting down at the weekends, he works for a civil engineering contractor. When it comes to Tonka toy driving, he is by all accounts very highly thought of. He has now bought his own machine, with a little help from me. It's a thirteen-ton Fiat-Hitachi.

Lorna has picked up more part-time lecturing at Bicton Agricultural College Exeter and has heard better news for after Christmas. In the new term she will pick up more hours at both colleges including evening classes at Bicton.

She has now got three horses in at livery for training. Better news still is that last year Lorna was asked to event a horse owned by a local business woman. Jane has now suggested she sponsors' Lorna for the coming year which means she will cover all the costs. Let's keep our fingers crossed for 1999.

That brings us up to date with my little darlings so where shall we turn our attention now.

RED AND CROSS

As has always been the case, nursing and my care continues to be a pain. Not the nurses themselves, but the authorities administering the system. When the policy of "care in the community" was introduced we hailed it as a triumph of common sense over adversity.

That was until we read the small print. There is a subtle but crucial paragraph that separates medical need from social need. Medical need is free at the point of delivery whereas social need has to paid for. My care has been determined as 50% medical and 50% social need. Devon County Council Social Services Department introduced a charging policy that has risen alarmingly since its inception. My argument is that, way back in 1974 at the high court, the opposition called witness evidence from the local health authority. They said in effect that they could provide nursing care to defeat my claim for compensation to provide my own nursing.

Since that time, you could say that the goal posts have been moved. I have contacted my barristers of the time (how's this for name dropping). The leading barrister is now Lord Chief Justice Oliver Popplewell and his then junior is now Chief Justice Philip Otton. Didn't do me any good though. Because the trial didn't set any legal precedents it was not recorded in the All-England Law Reports. I have learned that trial transcripts and recordings are destroyed after seven years. Consequently, I have no evidence to substantiate my claim for exemption from nursing charges. Don't stop me moaning though. Let's continue whinging.

GONNA MAKE YOU A STAR

The nurses that attend to my every need come from the local cottage hospital. Making headlines in the National Television News the Cornwall and Isles of Scilly Health Authority intend to close four local cottage hospitals in their area.

Not quite in the same league, but still making national headlines, was the fact that the North and East Devon Health Authority intend to close Lynton and Winsford (our local) cottage hospitals. The reason put forward was that they had overspent by some £2.2 million. Now obviously I have got a vested interest in Winsford staying open.

At a crowded public meeting attended by the quango (Quasi Autonomous Non-Government Organisation) faces, many people, including myself were quite vociferous in condemning any action that may result in the closure of such a valuable local asset.

The local Community Health Council and the Winsford League of friends obtained legal advice suggesting the N and E.D.H.A. had acted illegally. Judges in the High Courts in London confirmed THEY had exceeded their power by not consulting through the proper channels. Winsford is running within its set budget, the deficit being run up elsewhere.

When the judgement was handed down, BBC Southwest and Westcountry television wanted a face on screen to comment on the news. Sandra Willetts the chairperson of the league of friends was engaged elsewhere, so telephoned me to stand in (unfortunate turn of phrase). Before my giving an emotional plea to the camera, (Lawrence bloody Olivier move over), for the quango to think again, Janette was asked to push me past the hospital for introductory pictures. It was quite hysterical. We later learned the nurses inside the hospital were creased up watching us do several "takes" parading up and down.

Later we grabbed a few bystanders to make the protest look more authentic. Much later we congregated in numbers, this time with banners and local MP's for the benefit of the press. Much, much later we went on a march covering the parishes that Winsford serves. Since it was about twelve miles, I hasten to add I brought up the rear in my wagon picking up the stragglers. The embarrassing thing is, every time there is an update on the progress of the renewed consultation process, the TV wheel out their "library pictures" of Janette and me trolling up and down.

After all the efforts of the whole community THEY still went ahead with the closure which left everybody spitting nails. A triumph of accountants over common sense.

Now on a lighter note.

FOUR WEDDINGS AND A FUNERAL

You may recall that we lost (no, they died), our two Labradors. Zac and Gen. Janette replaced them with "Dotty" the Dalmatian. When "Dotty" reached the age of three Janette decided it would be nice to breed from her. A mate was duly selected after consulting the stud book and a 'wedding' arranged in August. "Buster" turned up on the day looking quite chipper. Unfortunately, Dotty gave him the run around and he cam... er... ejaculated to quickly and was sent home. Next day he arrived again, but was sent home in disgrace since he would not perform. I think he had been abusing himself overnight in frustration.

On the suggestion of Buster's owner, we then entered the big time. Charlie Watts, the drummer with the Rolling Stones (tongue in cheek-are you impressed at the circles we move in) has an estate in north Devon where he and his wife breed Arabian horses. The stud managers, Joan and Paul, have Dalmatian stud dogs. Dotty was introduced to Tonto. Tonto turned out to be too short (in the leg that is). Even though we stood him on a bank, he couldn't reach. Next the big guns were rolled out in the shape of the old but trusty Pancho.

Pancho lay down in the mid-day sun and wouldn't get up again. Even after a return visit the following day nothing was fourth coming. I mean that sincerely folks. We later heard poor old Pancho had expired. I'm not sure if it was too much heat or too much excitement.

On the suggestion of Joan, we were introduced to Arthur and Valentine Black. Newton Abbott was to be the venue. By this time Dotty was behaving like an absolute tart. Having learned what certain parts of her anatomy were for, she couldn't wait to put them to use. She had got her case packed and was waiting by the car door before dawn or whenever we showed signs of going out.

Boval Boomerang was sorry he ever met Dotty! With Arthur hanging on to Dotty's head and Valentine guiding the wedding tackle a union was made! ONE AND A QUARTER HOURS LATER Dotty finally let go of him. I'm sure it was with a sigh, and given the opportunity would have smoked a cigarette. Poor old Arthur who is no spring chicken was on his last knockings as well.

Starting at seven thirty in the morning, nine weeks later, attended by a bleary-eyed mid wife, Dotty produced eleven assorted puppies. Two liver spotted dogs, three liver spotted bitches, two black spotted dogs and four black spotted bitches! Even this animal neutral cynic was absolutely charmed by them. Even when we were up to the windowsills in piddle and shi… poo. Even for the next seven weeks until they were ready to go to their new homes. What a weird assortment of prospective owners we met during the selection process. Yes, it was a bit like interviewing candidates for Oxbridge. Everybody? Is looking forward to next June when we shall go through the whole process again.

Les Isted the chap who converted our house all those years ago (yes, we named the house after him) wasn't available to convert the coach house. Unfortunately, having built up a client base, he was unwilling to leave Ramsgate.

As for me, I try desperately to sit in the background quietly vegetating, rather like a voyeur of life. No chance I'm afraid. I seem to spend most of my time running a taxi service for the family. My other claim to fame is of course, my weight is increasing in direct inverse proportion to the rate of Janette's equally rapid diminishing height. In other words, as I get fatter Jan gets shorter.
ODDS AND SODS

Things to do next year. Give up smoking, <u>again!</u> Possibly sell the caravan. Rebuild the dining room chimney stack. Repair the dining room ceiling and redecorate. Render the outside walls and paint.

Decorate my bedroom. Redesign my bathroom to accommodate an ageing less mobile supercrip and redecorate. And on and on and on.

THE EPILOGUE

And finally. Enough of this I, me, we, us, our, and me, me, me. What a delight it was to receive your e-mail's and of course I would be so pleased to see any photographs (scanned or not) It will no doubt need to be said – How dare you both look so good. Which is why I am far too embarrassed to include any pictures of myself. However, Janette received a new camera for Christmas so depending on the results who knows!

With your news of Frans, Renee, Carl and Lesley I can almost picture them in the SA sun. The news of all the family's 'doings' is really good to hear. Do you feel like me? That having bought up the young 'uns. It gives one a certain satisfaction to see them on their way. Or am I just being an emotional old dork?

It goes without saying that if you can get over for the Rugby World Cup we really must meet up. Look. I think I've come to the end now. I'm running out of ideas. This has been fun; I must do it again when the inspiration strikes. But, after this six-week marathon I now need to lay down in a darkened room. Publish and be damned!   Regards! Naaaah! Love and best wishes for the New Year.

Alan J. Button. BBC News. Halwill. England. All written out. Exhausted. Bye.

THE PROLOGUE - SERIOUS STUFF!
Alan had started to write 'his' story. Unfortunately, it never got finished. But I wanted to add it for my readers now. In his own words: -

Subjects.

Introduce family. Work. Accident. Stoke. Stanmore. Leatherhead. Holidays. Move to Devon. House renovation.

Today is a good day. The sun is burning down out of a cloudless blue sky. The doors to the summerhouse are shut and the temperature inside soars to a drowsy but relaxing level. With chair tipped back and eyes closed it is easy to drift and reminisce about the past and how we arrived at this point in our lives.

It is now the summer of 2000, my name is Alan Button, I am 60 years old my wife is Janette and we have two children.

Back in 1969 we were, I like to think, go-ahead twenty some-things. July of that year saw us celebrate the birth of our second child, a daughter, Lorna. My son Gavin having been born in October 1965 was four.

I worked as Senior Technical Illustrator in the advertising department of B. Elliott and Company a large London engineering group who manufactured machine tools. I was involved in the production of illustrated parts lists and general advertising material.

On Thursday 13th November 1969 I left for work as usual. Swinging round the banister at the foot of the stairs, late as usual, I called goodbye to Janette and the children and drove my B reg. Vauxhall Viva the twelve miles down the Western Avenue to Gypsy Corner. Prophetically Janette's parting call was 'don't get involved moving those machines'.

It had been decided that on that particular morning the advertising and printing departments were to be transferred to new offices. John the print manager had made plans to obtain special hydraulic trolley jacks from Rotaprint for moving the printing machines. While he went off to get the jacks, I started to organise the move of the drawing boards and storage units of the advertising design department. When John came back, he said he had been unable to get the hydraulic jacks. However, the next best thing was to use castor wheels, these could be screwed into each corner of the base of the printing machines. This entailed levering the machines up using a crowbar so that the castor wheels could be attached. I was asked to help in this procedure. Whilst John levered up the machines I knelt down and attached the castors. It was then that the accident occurred, the machine toppled over and I was crushed underneath.

I cannot remember trying to move immediately after the incident but I was aware of considerable pain in my shoulder and neck area. I thought I had broken my collarbone. The factory nurse was the first medic on the scene. She placed a cushion under my head. When the ambulance drivers arrived, they first rolled me onto a blanket and then supervised my transfer onto a stretcher and then into the ambulance.

Taken by the ambulance to the Central Middlesex Hospital at Park Royal x-rays revealed I had broken my neck. A compression fracture of the fifth and sixth cervical vertebra had damaged my spinal cord leaving me paralysed.

I was given an injection and my memory of events became disjointed… My clothes were cut off…. A doctor explained I had broken my neck ….He was going to attach something to my skull to reduce the fracture.... He gave me a local anaesthetic in each temple.... He then drilled a hole on either side of my skull.... He then fixed a device to my head that looked like ice tongs....Onto which weights were fixed.... Janette appeared wearing hair curlers and pink chiffon head-scarf.... During the night I became desperately hot..... Someone close at hand was complaining about being only twenty-five percent. Was it me?.... Perhaps a reference to being an incomplete tetraplegic.... A female voice telling someone called Terry to keep still to avoid further damage. Was she talking to me?.... Then multi-coloured shapes the size of tea trays seemed to be fluttering about over me like bats...Oblivion.... I don't know what I was on, but it was a bad trip.

Following an overnight stay at CMH I was to be transferred to the National Spinal Injuries unit at Stoke Mandeville Hospital in Buckinghamshire.

However, the lifts chose this time to break down. I have intermittent memories of several events. I woke up on a stairwell landing surrounded by ambulance men who were manhandling the stretcher trolley and me to the ground floor.
I felt the cold air on my face as I was transferred to the waiting ambulance. I remember flashing lights; they were the neon lights of the Hanger Lane underpass.

I am told that the ride to Stoke Mandeville was quite an event in itself. We had an escort of police motorcycle outriders. They refused to allow anybody to overtake as the ambulance picked the smoothest route using all three lanes of the Western Avenue out of London at five thirty on a Friday evening. There must have been a lot of frustrated motorists waiting to get home that evening until we turned off onto the Aylesbury road.

We arrived at Stoke Mandeville Hospital late on Friday evening. The overhead corridor lights have been dimmed to a dull orange for the night. A nurse in a strange butterfly type starched headdress told us that this would be my home for the next nine months.

I was transferred by means of a sliding board onto an electrically operated bed, a strange machine more of which later. I fell deeply asleep until the usual bustle of hospital routine woke me the next morning.

A ward orderly rolled me onto my left side by sliding his hands under my chest and hips. I was trying to explain that the bed was electric but to no avail. The reason for the manhandling became apparent very shortly. Those readers of a nervous disposition should perhaps skip the next few sentences!

Despite my attempts to explain about the bed being electric, he commenced to turn back the bedclothes, apart from what was termed a modesty sheet and to my surprise and with no explanation, inserted two suppositories into my rectal passage. I was left to ponder my position for what seemed a considerable time before Manuel, for that was his name, returned and started to perform the first of many 'digital manual removal of faeces' from my bowel. After being cleaned up following this procedure I was rolled carefully onto my back.

A doctor appeared to introduce me to the next indelicate procedure which was to insert a catheter into my bladder via my penis to drain urine from my bladder. He explained this would be carried out three or four times a day until my bladder 'trained' itself to empty automatically. This was to set the scene for a daily routine that continues in various forms to this day.

This daily routine continued for the next twelve weeks interspersed with periods of physiotherapy in the form of passive movements of my paralysed limbs and occupational therapy

Thanks mainly to the combined efforts of 'my' physiotherapists Gail Bell (a South African voortrekker) and Leora Horovitz (a Lieutenant in the Israeli army) using the protocols devised by the late Sir Ludvic Guttman, they taught me or rather re-taught my revised body frame how to cope in its now foreign environment. After nine months of intensive therapy and rehabilitation in Stoke Mandeville Hospital I was discharged to face an uncertain future as a tetraplegic.

I attended Stanmore Orthopaedic Hospital daily as an outpatient to continue my rehabilitation where they encouraged me to think about returning to work and driving, although I had failed a medical test for a 'Noddy Car'.

I returned to work but found it impossible to continue. As a result of the nerve damage to my spinal cord, which not only inhibited my mobility, but also resulted in lack of manual dexterity, meaning I could not continue with my job of illustrating.

Also, at this time not only was Janette attending to our two under school-aged children, but she was doing the majority of the work involved in getting me up in the morning. Attending to my toileting, washing, dressing and all of the work involved in getting me into the car and driving me into London to work. A situation that could not be sustained and was resolved only when my car irreparably broke down.

I had started an action to claim damages for the injuries I had sustained in the accident, and in 1974 at the High Court in London Lord Chief Justice Waller awarded me damages for those injuries. Oliver Popplewell and Phillip Otton were leading and junior counsel respectively.

My attempts to find suitable employment compatible with my disability were to be enhanced by the Harrow Disabled Resettlement Office whose personnel suggested that it might help my chances of gainful employment if I took a course in book keeping.

However, one or two problems became apparent with the scheme. The first being that one of the requirements for book keeping at the time was reasonable hand writing. Another was the fact that the classes in book keeping were in a building that was entered via a flight of steps and were not wheelchair accessible.

I then spent a year at the Queen Elizabeth Training College for the Disabled near Leatherhead in Surrey where at the end of the course I took and passed an RSA examination in basic book keeping.

We started experimenting with holidays. Spending some interesting times at Motels, then package holidays in Portugal and Majorca and some weeks at an adapted Devon cottage.

In 1976, after disappointing attempts to find suitable employment, compatible with my disability, we were returning from a holiday in Devon to semi-detached suburbia when we made the decision to move away from London.

It would be an opportunistic time since both our children were at an age when they would be changing schools anyway.

We all sat down and discussed the plan and each wrote a specification of the ideal home that would make a move of this magnitude worthwhile.

It took us over year to find the right house and after many disappointments we were almost at the point of giving up. Staying at Hotels and Motels we had spent half terms, holidays and several long weekends looking for our 'ideal home'. Becoming increasingly desperate we had looked at everything from derelict farmhouses to 'barns with potential' to bungalows on estates and everything in between.

We had the details of one property to view and were debating whether it was worth travelling all that way to see just one house. We were still undecided the following morning when in the post we received the details of a second property. The Old Rectory at Halwill. Having two houses to view made the trip viable so we decided to go.

We had by this time worked out quite a good system of viewing properties.

Stage one was to drive up outside, look at the setting and in most case drive off again.

Stage two was to drive up outside and if we liked the setting Jan would have a quick recce inside.

Stage three was to drive up outside, like the setting and Jan approved the interior then she would get me out of the car into the wheelchair and into the house for a closer look.

The Old Rectory was the first on our list and was situated in the quiet backwater of Halwill in deepest rural Devon.

It was late Autumn and the country lane that led to the rectory was lined with lime and beech trees dressed in full finery.

Stage one was completed with nodded approval.

Stage two was completed when Jan came out after the briefest of interludes and breathlessly said 'I think we've found it'.

Stage three took much longer.

The house itself was a typical Victorian rectory. It was set on the brow of a low hill and surrounded on North, East and West sides by a mixture of mature trees. Sheltering but not overshadowing the house. The grounds were flat, giving level access. The front wrought iron gate with granite pillars gave into a circular gravelled drive.

Built of stone under a slate roof with the external walls rendered, large sash windows gave all the principal rooms, which faced south, plenty of light.

The front door on the East side gave into a lobby and through a half-panelled glass door lead into an 'L' shaped hall, stairs rose to the first floor with galleried landing.

Off the hall was a dining room, lounge, study and kitchen. Further rooms provided scullery, utility room, ground floor toilet, dairy and dry store. There was also internal access to a cellar.

On the first floor there were four bedrooms one with an adjoining bathroom, dressing room, a main bathroom and a further separate toilet.

Outside the grounds extended to about ten acres. Including a coach house, orchards, vegetable garden, paddocks and pastureland.

The overall impression was of a very sound family house in desperate need of some TLC, modernising and decorating.

The retired Reverend Dampier- Bennett, who was in residence, seemed to take great delight in showing us round the house and grounds even though at its sale he and his wife would be homeless.

He pointed out the best places to view the dramatic evening sunsets, the best places to have a bonfire and best places to go blackberry picking.

Later we investigated the immediate vicinity of the house. We discovered the primary school at the top of 'our' lane. In the village one and a half miles away, we found a cottage hospital, the local pub 'The Railway Inn' and the local garage. The nearest doctor's surgery was four miles away and the nearest market town nine miles away.

This really was the 'one'.

Unfortunately, the church commissioners would not accept an offer for the property insisting instead that it should be offered for sale at public auction. We retained a firm of local solicitors and set about getting expensive structural surveys done all with the prospect of not being the final bidder.

The Auction.

Joyce and John had agreed to look after the children for us while we went to Devon.
Stayed at 'The Devon Motel'. Travelled to Holsworthy next morning.
The auction was to be held at three o'clock in the function room of the 'White Hart Hotel'. We arrived far too early but that gave us time to have a look at the venue. Unfortunately, the function room was up

a flight of six steps and the bars were down another flight of steps.

Fortunately, Holsworthy was blessed with its fair share of watering holes so we went next door to the 'Crown' which had level access. Jan pushed me to the bar where I ordered sandwiches and drinks. We then found a quiet table and spent the next hour nervously studying the auction details over and over again.

As the time for the auction drew near, we moved back to the White Hart, where willing hands dragged my wheelchair up into the function room.

There were several lots to be auctioned 'ours' was the last.

For the next sixteen years we endeavoured to get on with the rest of our lives.

My children attended local schools, went to university and are now working in their chosen fields of Information Technology and College Lecturing.

For my part I was able to contribute to village and local life by being nominated and elected to serve on the local Playing Field, Village Hall and Pony Club committees, where I thoroughly enjoyed my time in office.

During this time my care needs were met mainly by the efforts of my wife supported twice a week by the District Nursing service.

When the National Health Service was re-organised, I was delighted to find my care was delegated to the staff of Winsford Hospital and I enjoyed several years of superb care and attention from them in my own home environment.

In 1993 with the introduction of the Care in the Community Act we were invited to attend a meeting to discuss my future care needs. An assessment of those needs was carried out.

At the meeting, the division between medical and social need was explained. It was further explained that my care requirements from then were determined as fifty per cent medical need and fifty per cent social need.

As you will be aware medical need is free at the point of delivery and social need is means tested.

I was not at all happy with the new proposals as it represented a complete 'moving of the goal posts' vis-à-vis commitments given in court (albeit by another party).

Agreement was reached, and instead of the two agencies (Health Authority and Social Services) providing a nurse and care assistant respectively, to carry out the differing roles, I was delighted to learn Winsford Hospital staff would undertake the whole care package. This was now to be delivered on alternate mornings with my wife attending to my needs for the rest of the time.

Provision was made, via the internal market, for the Health Authority to invoice Social Services for the time the Health Authority nurses were with me, but undertaking Social Services duties, and after an assessment of my resources I would be required to contribute towards the Social Services costs.

In practice the arrangement worked reasonably well, with again superb care and attention from the Winsford Hospital staff in my home environment.

You will be well aware of the current situation at Winsford Hospital and the various incidents leading to the closure. I observed at first hand the stress that the nursing staff, from Winsford, suffered as a result of the mis-handling of the situation by the Northern Devon Healthcare Trust, The North and East Devon Health Authority and the Community Health Council

In early 1998 an unfortunate incident occurred when one of the nurses required time off work after suffering a strained back muscle whilst helping transfer me to my wheelchair.

I presume that an accident report was filed and, as a result of that report an assessment of the nurses working environment, in our home, was carried out by Mr. John Simcox the Health and Safety Officer of the Northern Devon Healthcare Trust.

During the assessment my wife and I gave a practical demonstration of the procedures involved in getting me up in the mornings. Mr. Simcox concluded that the nurses were working in a 'high risk environment'.

On the orders of Mr. Simcox the protocols employed to deliver my care package have been completely revised.

Under the new regime two nurses are to be employed. They are to use a sliding board and sliding sheets to transfer me and a wheeled chair to propel me from bed to the facilities in an adjacent bathroom. This would avoid them contravening the guide-lines of the EC directive on manual handling.

My fear is that I will be in danger of losing my limited ability to stand and walk that is so essential to my wellbeing and our ability to manage the rest of our day when my wife alone has to stand and transfer me.

In practical terms it means my wish to make the best use of my limited ability to stand and walk will inevitably be diminished. If we try to overcome the shortcomings by creating artificial therapy during the day it will be physically more demanding on my wife who alone has to stand and transfer me.

On the face of it, the new regime would appear to be an easy option but it completely negates all the effort over the years to make best use of my limited ability to stand and walk.

I accept that in future I may well need extra staff to attend to my needs as time takes its toll on an ageing body, but not yet.

The nurses from Winsford Hospital recognised the shortcomings of the new protocols and expressed concern and then refused to implement them.

My care package was then transferred to the District Nursing Service of the Northern Devon Healthcare Trust and a team of Bank Nurses was set up to implement the new protocols.

As a secondary issue, Mr. Simcox has determined that an existing walk-in shower in the adjacent bathroom must be replaced by a wheel-in shower. This is to be provided from my own resources.

It would appear that if I accept the help offered by the District Nursing Service, I am obliged to accept the protocols introduced by the Health and Safety officer from the Northern Devon Healthcare Trust, as their employers.

Several months after the introduction of the new regime my worst fears were confirmed. It became apparent that I was developing mobility problems as a result of two carers lifting me.

I became increasingly concerned when several other incidents left me in doubt as to the effectiveness of the new regime and I started to look for an alternative solution.

I discovered that the Devon County Council Social Services department had implemented new legislation that allowed them to make direct payments to clients' willing and able to source their own care arrangements.

I made some enquiries and found a local care agency that could provide suitably trained staff to implement a care package tailored to my own preferred needs.

I have now set up a Direct Payment scheme and am delighted with the results. I have trained carers, I now know who is coming in, at what time and that they are working with me to promote increased mobility.

However, I have found a problem. The social services departments, under the new legislation, are unable to fund any care that is determined as medical need.

At present, my wife attends to my 'medical' need and the agency staff is attending to the 'social' need. This can lead to minor problems with timing.

I would like to relieve my wife of the burden of attending to me and the solution to this problem would be to allow the agency staff to cover both areas. They are willing and able to do this. It would seem the only way, at present, to achieve this is for me to pay the agency for my medical care.

I have approached the Northern Devon Healthcare Trust (copy enclosed) with a view to them funding my medical needs. This would ultimately save them money from their budget since they would not have to fund two nurses and their travelling expenses.

I have received a negative reply (copy enclosed) with a suggestion that I approach the North and East Devon Health Authority for funds since they are purchasers of healthcare.

It would appear that there is a lack of co-operation on the part of the medical agencies involved that is working against the spirit of the Community Care Act with protection of budgets the prime objective.

I have approached various bodies for assistance with funding, including the Independent Living Fund but find I am excluded for various reasons. I am running out of ideas.

I find it difficult to believe I am the only person in north Devon that requires both medical and social care in the community and because I choose not to use Health Authority staff and detrimental protocols I am having to pay for medical care.

Alan J. Button. BBC News. Halwill. England. All written out. Exhausted. Bye.

My name is... well it doesn't matter what my real name is.... But for the purpose of this exercise, I shall call myself Alistair St. John Butler. My problem is I want to die. I just don't have the courage to top myself because I am a coward. So, I have determined on a course of action. I am going to commit murder. Not just any murder but a vengeance spree against wrong doers. I shall be the arbiter of the victims.

This is as far as Alan's own story went.

BERNS BIT

Al, my old friend. We go back a long way, in what must have been the 50's, that we first met through your brother Malcolm. We would gather at your Mum and Dad's house (Mum and Dad Button to all of us). There would always be a houseful of us, 7 or 8, sometimes more and Mum Button would appear with an industrial sized plate of cheese sandwiches which we would all munch! It's to my shame that not one of us bought her a bunch of flowers as a thank you. My early memory of you is that you were always the quiet, thoughtful one and probably the cleverest of us all. We all had motorbikes, you, I remember, had an Ariel Colt and you had had explained to me you were going to turn it into an overhead cam model, from that moment on, I was in awe of you, it never happened, but it was the idea of it that amazed me! It was also your sense of humour that attracted me to you, you enjoyed the same sense of nonsense that I did. We continued to enjoy each other's company up to the time of the catastrophic accident, at which time we came close to Jan. Our relationship strengthened, by now of course Pauline had long joined our gang. This was such a turning point in your lives, two young children, a house which was a building site, and little or no future prospects, BUT a wife who was to stand by you and fight for and care for you to the end, small in stature but with enormous strength and fortitude (and boy, did she need that!) I remember our visits to you at Stoke Mandeville, you had weights attached to your head, only able to move your eyes, and a Social Worker coming around and saying "Any problems Mr Button?" You couldn't make it up! I also remember you keeping your sense of humour whilst in that state, and us both laughing with tears in our eyes over some silly joke or something. You eventually came home from Stoke Mandeville and I remember the offer to retrain you. You were taken to an address and it was up 2 flights of stairs!! The handrail on your stairs at home that came off the wall the first time you tried to use it! The nylon "sheepskin" you were given to stop you getting sore, we again, laughed ourselves silly recounting these tales. The story continues with your move to Devon and our joint friendship with Les, the builder, who also shared our sense of the ridiculous. With Jan's enormous help you fought your disability and as far as you both were able; you enjoyed your time in Devon. Lorna, as an adult then came into her own, and latterly supporting Jan, as she had supported you. You would be so proud of them both. Al, for all the problems you, Jan and Lorna fought, your love for your family was always evident, but my abiding memory is our silly sense of humour! Rest easy old friend, Bern and Pauline.

Lorna's Bit

How ironic that as I open a new word doc to add "my bit" (i.e., my recollections of my wonderful Dad), it's a document previously saved under that file name as a compilation of tributes by various people that wanted to pass on their thoughts about him as they remembered him in life and to give him a good "send off" at his funeral, which was a strictly private family affair.

"In the early hours of Thursday morning we sadly lost a truly inspirational man. Alan Button, husband of Janette and father to Gavin & Lorna, passed away in hospital.

Alan had suffered a lot in his life having been paralysed for 44 years and more recently he had been diagnosed with leukaemia. But despite all the challenges he faced on a daily basis, he still kept a smile on his face and a great sense of humour to go with it. He rarely let his paralysis stop him from doing things that we all take for granted, having a number of vehicles converted over the years to enable him to drive and get out to attend the various horse events that Lorna was competing in.

He even went up in a helicopter one year as a surprise birthday treat arranged by Gavin and the rest of the family!

Alan has touched many people's hearts over the years, but only those really close to him know what he had to endure everyday while still keeping a smile on his face.

Sir I salute you. Rest in Peace now Alan, we will never forget you........"

"Yesterday our small community lost a great man. Lots of words come to mind when I think of Alan Button, inspirational, outstanding, determined, likeable, humorous, the list goes on.... Paralysed some 44 years ago, with the help of his family he just got on with life, doing things that many able-bodied people would never attempt. All those words sum him up, but don't quite do it, then I realized that whenever I spoke to him or met him driving on the road (in the past driving a bloody great American motorhome with a big horse box attached) when he was gone, I'd always shake my head & say what a f*"%ing amazing Bloke. RIP Alan"

"I always admired his cheerfulness despite his difficulties. He was a fighter through and through. The world will be a quieter place without him. My children will always have wonderful memories of Alan and his "groovy" wheels. He was an amazing man and fought so bravely against his illness. The sheer determination he had I've never seen before. He has been inspirational by demonstrating what can be done in spite of the hurdles of disability.

Such a kind and caring man. Sparkling intelligence, eloquence and wonderful sense of humour. A truly inspirational Gentleman"

"I was truly impressed with how he handled the life that was placed in front of him. Great guy!!!!"

"I have such fond memories of a man who was so caring and upbeat with a great sense of humor.... never complaining about the hand he was dealt. He handled himself with such dignity."

"One day someone is going to hug you so tight. That all of your broken pieces will stick back together.

Hey ho, probably not the best prologue, or whatever it is correctly termed, for the start of "my bit!"

But something's have to be said….

Of course, every daughter thinks their Dad is the greatest in the world, but to hear people's true thoughts of my Dad and how he handled the life that had been dealt to him is truly humbling. Its lovely to know that people thought and admired him as much as I did. It's still strange and sad to refer to him in the past tense, even though it's now 6 years since we lost him as I write this.

So, November 13th 1969, our world was transformed. Note the phrasing, "our world was transformed" not "our world ended".

Needless to say, I have no recollection of "that" day. But suffice to say life would never be the same.

I can't even begin to comprehend the trauma that was about to unfold...... talk about ignorance is bliss...... You're whole world imploding.... although I doubt Mum & Dad knew the extent of the "implode" at that time.

Talk about "wrong place, wrong time". I won't go into details of the "accident" – suffice to say outcome was c5/c6 SCI (spinal cord injury) – Google it – it's not good!

But hey, I'm 4 months old – what difference does that make to me - not a lot. To my brother, who is 4 years older, it must have been "universe dropping out of" scene – Dad doing usual things with 4-year-old son – suddenly not any more - how horrific.

& how about your new wife?! That wasn't mentioned in the contract! The ultimate respect for "guerding of loins" ...... unbelievable the "you're on your own" scenario awaiting us!

As for law courts, fortunately my late father had a brain and a "terrier" of a wife when it came to seeking compensation for this catastrophe! The 1st solicitor was a wet lettuce; then they got the "big boys". 4 years later (with f*ck all income in the meantime) the damages claim was won. Next issue – getting staff to look after his incredibly complex care needs.

This would be an ongoing issue throughout Dads life....

Without going into details & degrading my Dad further....... Imagine not being able to have a shit unaided - & no we are not talking some suppositories and waiting... we're talking manual lower bowel evacuation.

The majority of this DAILY care was left to his wife, my mum.... Would you be prepared for this "through sickness and in health" – yea it's easy to say for a 1 off, but 44 years???

As Dad was a highly skilled draughtsman (before the advent of CAD) as his career in London, to continue this employment post injury was fascicle, so, staying in London became an "issue".

It was decided to leave the "rat race" and establish a new life elsewhere. On the wish list were Australia (Mum) and South Africa (Dad). The logistics of such a monumental move were a stretch too far, so, after 3 years of searching, the new home in Halwill, Devon was purchased. Well, I say purchased.... Mum & Dad had to attempt to buy the selected property at auction in a kinda "shit or bust" scenario! & there the "fun" began!

"Newbies" – let's see what profit we can make outta these guys! & screw us they did!

But eventually, due to an awesome builder friend who "didn't take any shit" and resilience you would not believe from Mum & Dad – we moved in to the Old Rectory at Halwill. The sales particulars stated that it was in need of modernisation – slight understatement in the sales particulars! But it was the ideal blank canvas to adapt it for Dad's needs; as the preferred option of the "powers that be" to bundle us all into a kind of "disabled commune" after the injury was a complete NO GO for Mum and Dad.

The "circus" that confronted the "locals" as we descended must have been phenomenal & apart from a few "un-PC" comments from our immediate neighbours ("Alan walks funny like that Great Dane up the road" ....) & that's the polite ones(!), we landed at our new country home – which was and still is my home 40 plus years later!

I must admit to initially not being overly impressed with our new home – it smelt funny!! Plus, I'd left all my friends back in Harrow – stamps foot in truly obnoxious brat-like child manner!!! But on the plus side, it was looking hopeful that I may actually get a pony of my own! Whoops in again truly obnoxious brat-like child manner!!

Although soon I too fell in love with the place (new pony aside!) as well and it wasn't long before my old life in Harrow was happily replaced by my new country life, with new friends and a pony to boot! So much so that when I moved away to work as part of this rather tedious bit of having to grow up and become an adult, the lure of "home" was always incredibly strong – and here I still am! I truly embraced my new country life and loathe having to leave it! Indeed, I think people thought I must have got my braces caught in Halwill, as I kept coming home!

But for all the hurdles – we tried to find solution…. So much so that some of the hurdles were so high, most "able bodied" peeps ran away…….

Hence my admiration and inspiration of Dad was immense. As was the respect! Being disabled meant there was never any threat of a "smacked arse" from him – yes those were the days when if you're "little darlings" stepped out of line there were going to be consequences! But I respected him totally. I don't even recall him raising his voice. It was enough to know that I didn't want to disappoint, embarrass or cause further hassle in his already stressful life, that I towed the line – well most of the time....!

I can honestly say I never saw Dad show any reticence about the cruel twist of fate he had to deal with. He was always cheerful, polite and patient. He had a wonderful sense of humour and was highly intelligent and practical. This must have been immensely frustrating for him as he had to watch able bodied people (especially myself (I was particularly "cack handed" with practical stuff as I am left-handed) and Mum) make tasks he would have dealt with and completed in minutes, take hours and usually end up going "Pete Tong"! On the plus side, it made both Mum and I pretty independent and strong willed, as we did not have an able-bodied man to do a lot of the jobs that need doing about the place. Although anything to do with engines and mechanics is still a mystery to me! As is the rugby scrum! What is all that about??!! As Dad used to play rugby, we enjoyed watching premiership and international rugby matches together, but I never "got" the scrum!!

I like to think that Dad and I had a very strong bond and still miss his kind and guiding words of wisdom.

I still recall the day before he died going to a competition with the last homebred horse out of his brood mare. Only to return home later that day to be met by his carer who was there to whisk me back to the hospital as the "end was close". I was in total shock and definitely would not have been in a fit state to drive. Thankfully a friend had come with me to the competition, so she kindly dealt with the horse and told me to get to the hospital ASAP. I didn't change clothing, so rocked up to the hospital in competition breeches and shirt and reeking of "eau de cheval", sweat etc! Unfortunately, by the time I got there he was unconscious and not even my smelly presence would awaken him, but I hope he knew I was there with him.

Anyway, enough doom, gloom and despondency! Yes, life was different and tough at times, but I have inherited my Dads "glass half full" mantra. Even though my Dad was severely disabled, at least his was still in my life – unlike some friends whose parents were estranged/divorced or rarely saw their Dads due to their work or had to endure the horrible fate of losing their Dad for some reason.

I have a memory bank full of wonderful times and experiences, some of which would probably not have occurred if the injury hadn't happened.

When we went out for a meal (not a regular occurrence), we would inevitably make a grand entrance! Usually, first by either being hauled unceremoniously up the entrance steps, or by trying to improvise a ramp to enter the premises (before DAS was in place) and then rearranging most of the tables and furniture to allow Dad to gain access to our table! I do so hate exhibitionists!! This was despite the first question always being "is your premises wheelchair accessible?". Many people genuinely don't understand the extent of "wheelchair friendly" or the requirements of a wheelchair user. Still, it was always an ice-breaker and conversation starter with other diners!! Usually much to my brothers and mum's embarrassment! Hence, I think I became a bit of an extrovert! Cue the VHS of our Okehampton College 6th form panto of Snow White and the 7 dwarves!! And yes, it was my Dad shouting all the usual panto audience engagement phrases of "Oh no he's not! He's behind you! Boo, hiss!" etc etc. Much to the hilarity of the rest of the parent audience and my fellow cast members!

I have such happy memories of my life with Dad. I guess we experienced the same ups and downs as other families, but these were in no way due to his "condition". I'm sure some probably were, but that's not my recollection. There were very few occasions we had to "admit defeat" due to his paralysis as he was always so determined not to allow his family to be compromised because of his disability. You only experience 1 childhood and yes, I'm sure mine was probably different in some ways but I knew no different. My Dad had always had "wheels", so I knew/saw no difference.

Through into adulthood I had the same rollercoaster ride as many and I was always grateful to be able to rely on Dads words of wisdom/comfort, both through the highs and the lows. I hope I did him proud. RIP awesome gentlemen AKA Dad xx

<u>Gavins Bit</u>

Recollections of my dear dad
Funny how the human memory works isn't it. Some recollections of my dear dad are as clear as day, others slightly faded or incomplete. Even now when I look back, I have to try hard to catalogue them all

in the correct chronological order so as to not miss any anecdotes or misquote events altogether. It's a good job in today's world with the wonders of our computer integrated life we can so easily insert a paragraph into a letter which we first forgot. No messing around with Tipp-ex or starting afresh from scratch. Pity we can't do this for real life.
I realise now by putting these memories down on paper how many times dad amazed and enlightened me with new and fascinating ideas. His sense of humour and his relentless number of "dad" jokes although old to the rest of the world but new to me would always have me in giggling fits.
Yellow dinkey car transporter and the phone call
It was November 1969 and I was 4 years old. I'd just had my lunch and was looking forward to a hard afternoon slog of driving my dinkey car transporter up and down the hallway at Westward avenue. The hallway had a dark brown carpet which made the bright yellow dinkey toy almost fluorescent in contrast. The phone rang and mum came bustling out from the kitchen heading towards the phone near the front door. In the process she elegantly sidestepped me laying on the floor and just brushed the dinkey toy with the heal of her foot. "Do you mind madam; this is a six-lane public highway and you have impeded my vehicle without due care or attention" I exclaimed. In reality what came out of my gob as a 4-year-old was "Brrrrr. Screech, honk, honk!".
I can't recollect the words in the telephone conversation but even as a young child I realised

this was serious news. Mums vocal tones were getting more agitated as the conversation progressed so much so that I even stopped playing, sat up and just looked at her intently. The call ended and my sister Lorna and I were bundled off to dear Joyce and John Bathard who lived a few doors up. Mum meanwhile was rushing off the hospital to find out the severity of dad's accident.

Open sesame

Weeks later I was allowed to visit dad in hospital. It was quite a long journey for all of us, this was well before the age of DVD's and computer games to keep me occupied. The I spy game only lasted 10 minutes before the familiar phrase "Are we nearly there yet?" was muttered. A phrase that would become an in joke for the family in later years with our numerous journeys from London to Devon. Stoke Mandeville hospital was a specialised hospital for spinal cord injuries and had been equipped with the latest gadgets including automatic doors which were my first encounter of such a delight. As we walked up to the entrance, lo and behold the doors opened without having to push or pull a handle. Brilliant. As we progressed down the corridor more automatic doors. I started running to see if I was quick enough to beat the doors opening. Mum quickly realised my game and hauled me in by the arm. Game over, busted.

At last, we reached the ward where dad was. On entering I was met by two rows of beds that seem to go on forever. Glancing left I spot dad looking at me from a prone position and instantaneously both our faces light up in delight to see each other. As I get closer, I am intrigued by all the pipes and tubes and metal frame that supports his neck. I innocently ask dad if they take the bars from out of his neck will his head fall off? to which both mum and dad both laughs.
Future visits to the hospital involve a tour by dad to the gym where he has his physio therapy sessions. He is now in a wheel chair and I have my first go at pushing him down the corridor of the hospital. Left a bit right a bit, right a bit I say to myself whilst peering over dads' shoulder from behind the chair. What could possibly go wrong! I think we were both a bit anxious on that first trip only topped when some 12 years later when we find ourselves in a similar situation. I was learning to drive with dad in the passenger seat gripping the car door handle as best he could and quoting the highway code at me in a nervous high-pitched voice.
Christmas under the table
Time passed and dad was eventually allowed home for the first Christmas. Because the house did not have any modifications yet for dad's new lifestyle hew was confined to the ground floor and the dining room converted to his bedroom. This didn't bother me but must have been a bit of a juggling act for both mum and dad. This Christmas there seemed to be more presents than usual, presumably

because of the sympathy from all those around the family. All the presents were piled up under the dining table from where my Lorna and myself would be opening them.

This is the Christmas where I get my first Hornby train set and I look to dad to fix it all together for me. This was of course impossible due to the lack of dexterity afforded to dad by the accident. So, with patient verbal instructions from dad, I connected the pieces of track together to form a simple oval shape together with a station platform. This was the first of many such projects between dad and myself. On reflection I now realise this was a learning curve for both of us. Not only for me to interpret these instructions but for dad to orchestrate them verbally without one or both of us losing the plot.

Boy allowed to use grown up tools

As weeks went on, I undertook more of the menial DIY tasks around the house which inevitably involved dad again patiently instructing me how to use knives, saws, screwdrivers, hammers and drills. I'm sure mum scorned dad for letting me use some of those tools and yes there were a few cuts, bruises and tears but we avoided any trips to A&E and what a way to learn!

It was probably this early baptism of fire of dad's toolbox which led me to the career of mechanical, electrical, software engineer and general fix anything guy that I am today. Thanks, dad, for all those patient instructions in those early years.

How does that work Part 1? The Lego gearbox

A few years passed and the family unit adapted to dad's new lifestyle. One of my schooling tasks each Saturday morning was to learn my times tables. Mum had written down the tables on a bit of spare wall paper and Sellotaped it the inside of my wardrobe door. I was tasked to recite these tables in front of mum and dad before being allowed to watch TV, the highlight of this was Noel

Edmonds and the Multicoloured swap shop. With the onerous task done I duly nipped downstairs to turn on the TV. Horror no power in the house. I think this was when the coal miners were on strike and power blackouts in London where common at that time.

I had to find something else to do with my Saturday morning, so without further ado I opened my box of Lego and started to build a buggy. An hour or so later I had a motorised 4-wheel vehicle, when switched on it trundled along the bedroom floor at a rather unimpressive sedate pace. Hmm how do I make it go faster? I thought. "Dad how do I make it go faster" I shouted from my bedroom. I took the box of Lego and the buggy to see dad and explained the problem. He cast an eye over the pieces and without hesitation tells me I need to build a gearbox. Up to that point I didn't know what a gearbox was, but within a few minutes we had constructed a rudimentary 3 speed gearbox. Just by sliding the position of one driveshaft left or right was enough to change gears. To this day I am still amazed at the ingenuousness of this simple design which dad thought up in a blink of an eye. Respect. Mind. Mind. Mind!

It was one of those hot summer evenings and the family had decided to eat tea on the patio in the back garden. I was sitting in a chair facing away from the garden and realised I could easily rock it backwards and forwards as kids do by folding my legs under the front of it. What I hadn't realised every time I did this the chair was creeping closer and closer to the edge of the Patio. I was now becoming bolder with this newly found rocking/balancing act.

Suddenly dad shouted at me "Mind", what? I thought and started another rock. Then in unison both mum and dad shouted "mind". OK, I thought I can handle this new party trick and started another rock this time to far. Now all, mum, dad and Lorna shouting "Mind" as the two rear chair legs slipped off the edge of the patio catapulting me backwards into one of the flower beds. Hey presto another family saying was invented.

How does that work Part 2? The technical illustrator Dad had now been compensated for the accident and we had moved to Devon. I had started secondary school and had been tasked with designing a hook for a saw for my metalwork class as homework. The remit from school was to produce a drawing with enough specification to produce the hook.

I set to work with pencil and paper attempting to draw something that I thought was feasible to produce. After several attempts and lots of rubbing out I noticed dad was watching me. "What you doing?" has asked. I explained the task at hand to which his eyes just lit up.

Before the accident dad was a technical illustrator. This sort of thing you would find in a Haynes manual with exploded views of engine assemblies etc. My homework task was exactly the kind of thing he had done for a living.

From behind dads' desk was hauled an old and dusty drawing board complete with auto levelling straight rule. I dusted it off and attached a brand-new piece of A4 paper. This bit of homework was going to be so cool I thought. Over the course of the next few hours dad yet again patiently explained the concepts of first and third angle projection, projection lines and how to dimension a

drawing with appropriate datums. I think we were both impressed with the end result which I proudly handed in to Mr Parkinson the metalwork teacher on Monday morning.
I don't think the teacher was expecting such an elaborate piece of work from a 14-year-old and even though I could explain it in meticulous detail he didn't believe it was my own work and gave me a rather low mark for all that hard effort. I think humility is what this exercise taught me, yet another trait that dad had passed onto me with his typical libra manner. God bless you dad.

The acoustics of Isted house

Our home in Devon was a large old building with big thick walls. On many occasion family members would shout to each other rather than making the journey to the next room and asking the question in person. Simple things like "Cup of tea?" would be met with silence or "What?". We could find ourselves repeating the question in increasingly louder volumes until one or both partners gave up or made the journey to the other room. One such occasion I was working on my motorbike in the garage and came into the empty kitchen.
"Mum, where's my Yamaha manual" I shouted. Silence. Increasing the volume, I asked the question again. "Where's who's hammer" mum shouted back. Totally flummoxed at trying to interpret mum's response. "What?" I shouted back. Dad now entering into a three-way conversation who must have been between us both and herd

both sides of the conversation exclaimed to us in a loud voice "It's the glue sticks". Neither of us could fathom this response from dad, I mean how did glue sticks relate to my bike manual? It transpires what dad had shouted back to us was "it's the acoustics of the house". Yet again another family saying was inspired.

Appendix

Spinal cord injury (SCI) involves damage to the nerves within the bony protection of the spinal canal. The most common cause of SCI is trauma, although damage can occur from various diseases acquired at birth or later in life, from tumors, electric shock, poisoning or loss of oxygen related to surgical or underwater mishaps.

A common misconception is that a spinal cord injury means the spinal cord has to be severed in order for a loss of function to occur. In fact, most people who have sustained a SCI, the spinal cord is bruised and intact.

The spinal cord and the brain together make up the central nervous system (CNS). The spinal cord coordinates the body's movement and sensation. Therefore, an injured cord loses the ability to send and receive messages from the brain to the body's systems that control sensory, motor, and autonomic function below the level of injury. Often, this results in some level of paralysis.

Spinal cord trauma is more than a single event. The initial blunt force damages or kills spinal nerve cells. However, in the hours and days after injury a cascade of secondary events, including loss of oxygen and the release of toxic chemicals at the site of injury, further damage the cord.

Acute care following an injury may involve surgery if the spinal cord appears to be compressed by bone, a herniated disk, or a blood clot. Traditionally, surgeons waited for several days to decompress the spinal cord, believing that operating immediately could worsen the outcome. More recently, many surgeons advocate immediate early surgery.

Generally speaking, after the swelling of the spinal cord begins to go down, most people show some functional improvement after an injury.

With many injuries, especially incomplete injuries (some motor or sensory function preserved below the injury level), a person may recover function eighteen months or more after the injury. In some cases, people with SCI regain some function years after the injury.
There is a lot of information and resources to learn about the effects of a spinal cord injury. However, it is important to understand the functions of the spinal cord and its relationship to the brain.

Understanding the spinal cord

The spinal cord includes neurons and long nerve fibres called axons. Axons in the spinal cord carry signals downward from the brain (along descending pathways) and upward toward the brain (along ascending pathways).

Many axons in these pathways are covered by sheaths of an insulating substance called myelin, which gives them a whitish appearance. Therefore, the region in which they lie is called "white matter." Loss of myelin, which can occur with cord trauma and is the hallmark of such diseases as multiple sclerosis, prevents effective transmission of nerve signals.

The nerve cells themselves, with their tree-like branches called dendrites that receive signals from other nerve cells, make up "gray matter." This gray matter lies in a butterfly-shaped region in the center of the spinal cord.

Like the brain, the spinal cord is enclosed in three membranes (meninges):

- Pia mater: Innermost layer
- Arachnoid: Delicate middle layer
- Dura mater: Tougher outer layer.
  The spinal cord is organized into segments along its length, noted by their position along the thirty-three vertebrae of the backbone. Nerves from each segment connect to specific regions of the body, and thus control motor and autonomic functions.

In general, the higher in the spinal column an injury occurs, the more function a person will lose.

Cervical region
The segments in the neck, or cervical region, referred to as C1 through C8, control signals to the neck, arms, hands, and, in some cases, the diaphragm. Injuries to this area result in tetraplegia, or as it is more commonly called, quadriplegia.

- Injury above the C3 level may require a ventilator for the person to breathe.
- Injury above the C4 level usually means loss of movement and sensation in all four limbs, although often shoulder and neck movement is available to facilitate sip-and-puff devices for mobility, environmental control, and communication.
- C5 injuries often spare the control of shoulder and biceps, but there is not much control at the wrist or hand. Those at C5 can usually feed themselves and independently handle many activities of daily living.
- C6 injuries generally allow wrist control, enough to be able to drive adaptive vehicles and handle personal hygiene, but those affected at this level often lack fine hand function.

Thoracic region
Nerves in the thoracic or upper back region (T1 through T12) relay signals to the torso and some parts of the arms.

- Injuries from T1 to T8 usually affect control of the upper torso, limiting trunk movement as the result of a lack of abdominal muscle control.
- Lower thoracic injuries (T9 to T12) allow good trunk control and good abdominal muscle control.

Lumbar and sacral regions

- Those injured in the lumbar, or mid-back region just below the ribs (L1 through L5), are able to control signals to the hips and legs.
- A person with an L4 injury can often extend the knees.
- The sacral segments (S1 through S5) lie just below the lumbar segments in the mid-back and control signals to the groin, toes, and some parts of the legs.
Besides a loss of sensation or motor function, injury to the spinal cord leads to other changes, including loss of bowel, bladder, and sexual function, low blood pressure, autonomic dysreflexia (for injuries above T6), deep vein thrombosis, spasticity, and chronic pain.

Other secondary issues related to injury include pressure ulcers, respiratory complications, urinary tract infections, pain, obesity, and depression.

These complications of a spinal cord injury are mainly preventable with good healthcare, diet, and physical activity.

Cells that control spinal cord function

Several types of cells carry out spinal cord functions, including:

- Large **motor neurons** have long axons that control skeletal muscles in the neck, torso, and limbs.
- **Sensory neurons** called dorsal root ganglion cells, or afferents, carry information from the body into the spinal cord and are found immediately outside the spinal cord.
- **Spinal interneurons**, which lie completely within the spinal cord, help integrate sensory information and generate coordinated signals that control muscles.
- **Glia**, or supporting cells, far outnumber neurons in the brain and spinal cord and perform many essential functions.
- One type of glial cell, the **oligodendrocyte**, creates the myelin sheaths that insulate axons and improve the speed and reliability of nerve signal transmission.
- **Astrocytes**, large star-shaped glial cells, regulate the composition of the fluids that surround nerve cells. Some of these cells also form scar tissue after injury.
- Smaller cells called **microglia** also become activated in response to injury and help clean up waste products.

All of these glial cells produce substances that support neuron survival and influence axon growth. However, these cells may also impede recovery following injury; some glial cells become reactive and thereby contribute to formation of growth-blocking scar tissue after injury.

Nerve cells of the brain and spinal cord respond to trauma and damage differently than most other cells of the body, including those in the peripheral nervous system (PNS). The brain and spinal cord are confined within bony cavities that protect them, but this also renders them vulnerable to compression damage caused by swelling or forceful injury.

Cells of the CNS have a very high rate of metabolism and rely upon blood glucose for energy – these cells require a full blood supply for healthy functioning; therefore, CNS cells are particularly vulnerable to reductions in blood flow (ischemia).

Other unique features of the CNS are the "blood-brain-barrier" and the "blood-spinal-cord barrier." These barriers, formed by cells lining blood vessels in the CNS, protect nerve cells by restricting entry of potentially harmful substances and cells of the immune system.

Trauma may compromise these barriers, potentially contributing to further damage in the brain and spinal cord. The blood-spinal-cord barrier also prevents entry of some therapeutic drugs.

Complete vs. incomplete SCI

What is the difference between a complete injury and an incomplete injury?

Those with an incomplete injury have some sensory or motor function below the level of injury – the spinal cord was not totally damaged or disrupted. In a complete injury, nerve damage obstructs all signals coming from the brain to the body below the injury.

While there's almost always hope of recovering some function after a spinal cord injury, it is generally true that people with incomplete injuries have a better chance of getting more return.

The sooner muscles start working again, the better the chances are of additional recovery. When muscles come back later, after the first several weeks, they are more likely to be in the arms than in the legs.

As long as there is some improvement and additional muscles recover function, the chances are better that more improvement is possible. The longer there is no improvement, the lower the odds it will start to happen on its own.

SCI stats

A study from the Reeve Foundation estimates that over 1.2 million Americans are living with paralysis resulting from spinal cord injuries – five times the previous commonly used estimate of 250,000.

A sample of the insights gleaned from the research on the prevalence of SCI include:

- About four out of five people with spinal cord injuries are male.
- More than half of spinal cord injuries occur in the cervical area, a third occur in the thoracic area, and the remainder occur mostly in the lumbar region.
- Spinal cord injuries are most commonly caused by motor vehicle accidents, followed by sports-related injuries (more common in children and teenagers), falls and acts of violence.
These findings have major implications for the treatment of spinal cord and paralysis-related diseases – not only for those living with these conditions, but also for their families, caregivers, healthcare providers, and employers.

People who sustain a spinal cord injury are mostly in their teens or twenties, although as the population in general ages, the percentage of older persons with paralysis is increasing.

As the number of people living with paralysis rise and as they age with the injury, the costs associated with treating them increase as well. Each year, paralysis costs the healthcare system billions of dollars. Spinal cord injuries alone cost roughly $40.5 billion annually – a 317 percent increase from costs estimated in 1998 ($9.7 billion).

People living with paralysis and spinal cord injuries are also often unable to afford health insurance that adequately covers the complex secondary or chronic conditions that are commonly linked with paralysis.

Research and scientific developments

Currently, there is no cure for spinal cord injuries. However, ongoing research to test surgical and drug therapies is progressing rapidly. Injury progression prevention drug treatments, decompression surgery, nerve cell transplantation, nerve regeneration, and complex drug therapies are all being examined as a means to overcome the effects of spinal cord injury.

The Reeve Foundation has been leading the charge in spinal cord research for over 30 years, creating a framework to translate scientific breakthroughs into vital new therapies. Additionally, we have established programs to help cultivate the next generation of researchers that will safeguard a pipeline of innovation across the field and speed the delivery of cures for spinal cord injury.

Spinal Cord Injury: What is it and what does it affect? May 2018 Author: Shirley Ryan AbilityLab - Spinal Cord Injury Team The spinal cord is like a great telephone communications system made of millions of nerves that carry messages between the brain and all parts of the body. It is surrounded by bony rings called vertebrae. The column of nerves and bones that travel from the brain to the tail bone make up the spinal cord. The protective bony structure is the spinal column. An injury to the spinal column may cause the bones around the spinal cord to break and press against the spinal cord, causing damage to nerves. Damage to the spinal cord and nerves can happen without damage to the bones. Many nerves lead from the brain through the spinal cord to the skin, muscles, and organs of the body. These nerves enter and exit the spinal cord at specific levels and each level goes to specific parts of the body. The first seven levels are called cervical levels; they control breathing, neck, and arm function. Next are the twelve thoracic levels. These nerves are responsible for the chest and torso areas. The five lumbar levels are next and control the legs. Last are the sacral levels that are involved in bowel, bladder, sexual, and leg function. It is through these nerves that the brain tells the body to move. Nerves operate along a pathway (the spinal cord); when the path is broken the messages cannot get through. This occurs when there is an injury or disease of the spinal cord. Following damage to the spinal cord the levels above the damage continue to work but all levels below the damage will be affected. Complete vs. Incomplete The degree of loss of body function following injury or disease to the spinal cord depends on the level and "completeness" of the injury. The completeness of the injury refers to the amount of messages that are traveling through the spinal cord. If there is no feeling or movement below the level of injury, it is considered a complete injury. If there is some feeling or movement well below an injury level then it is an incomplete injury. Initially after an injury the nerves are "in shock." There is swelling around the spinal cord, much like any other part of your body that swells when injured. As the swelling begins to decrease, there may be some improvement in body function below the injury level. This is how a spinal cord injury affects body functions. Skeletal System Right after injury, some calcium and minerals often leave the bones. Eventually, these may deposit in the urinary system causing stones (calculi). Getting out of bed and moving around as soon as advised will help prevent this; so, for this and other important reasons, therapists try to get you out of bed and as active as possible. Because you cannot move about as you used to, joints (knees, elbows, shoulders, etc.) may become stiff. This is why you have range of motion exercises (ROM). You can help keep full movement of your joints by correct positioning in bed and by doing as much of your self-care as possible. Urinary Tract System The urinary system is made up of kidneys (which filter the blood and produce urine) and the bladder (which holds and then gets rid of the urine). After a spinal cord injury, the kidneys continue to make urine but the bladder may not work as before. You may be unable to tell when your bladder is full or you may not be able to push the urine out when necessary. The bladder may hold the urine and a catheter may be needed to empty it or the urine may come out without your wanting it to, causing urinary accidents. There are different types of catheters, medication, and other techniques that can promote independence with emptying your bladder. Therapists work with you to find ways to manage your urinary system. but the bladder may not work as before. You may be unable to tell when your bladder is full or you may not be able to push the urine out when necessary. The bladder may hold the urine and a catheter may be needed to empty it or the urine may come out without your wanting it to, causing urinary accidents. There are different types of catheters, medication, and other techniques that can promote independence with emptying your bladder. Therapists work with you to find ways to manage your urinary system. Bowels The digestive system breaks down the food you eat. After a spinal cord injury, digestion continues but the ability to control bowel movements may be affected. When the rectum becomes full, a message is sent to the brain which then tells you to wait until you can get to a bathroom. Following a spinal cord injury, messages may not get to the brain so there may be a problem in stopping or starting a bowel movement. Depending on the level of injury, you may not have use of the abdominal (stomach) muscles which help push the stool out. Bowel accidents, constipation, and impaction can occur. After a new spinal cord injury, you will have to re-train your bowels. A new routine including different techniques, methods, and medications can help you regain normal bowel elimination. Developing a new bowel program will prevent accidents, and promote regular bowel movements. Nurses work with you to develop a bowel program. Skin protects the body from the outside world by making it hard for bacteria and germs to enter the body. The spinal cord serves as an important messenger to your skin to protect it from being hurt. For example, when you sit in one position for a long time you begin to feel uncomfortable and shift or move around in your chair; this helps prevent sores from developing. After a spinal cord injury, you may no longer feel the discomfort and not move around, putting yourself at risk for a pressure sore (bed sore). If sores develop, the skin is open and germs can enter the body, increasing risk for serious infections. There are many ways to change positions, and to be aware of possible skin problems before they occur. Skin checks and skin care can be discussed with your nursing team. Pressure relief exercises will help protect your skin. Respiratory System Lungs are the major organ involved in breathing and these are not affected by spinal cord injury. However, being able to move air in and out of the lungs depends on muscles. So, depending on the level of the injury, being able to cough or take deep breaths may be affected. The most important muscle in breathing is the diaphragm. This is a large dome-shaped muscle that is directly below the lungs. If a spinal cord injury is at cervical 4 or higher, a machine or ventilator may be necessary to help with breathing. Additional airway problems exist in spinal cord injuries at this level. Coughing and deep breathing is a way to fully expand and open your lungs to keep them moving and healthy. The thoracic levels help make the cough strong and lungs clean. There are things you can do to help keep your lungs healthy. If your injury is below thoracic 6 and you are active you will probably not notice any changes in your ability to breathe. A good tool for any person staying in the hospital setting is called the incentive spirometer. It is a tool that makes you take deep breaths, opening up your lungs and helping them stay clear and healthy. Autonomic Function The autonomic nervous system consists of nerves controlled by the brain and spinal cord that run both inside and outside the spinal cord. This system controls glands, digestion, heart, temperature and blood pressure among others. After a spinal cord injury some of these functions may be affected, such as temperature and blood pressure regulation. This is particularly true if the injury has occurred at thoracic 6 or above. Normally when you go out in very cold or hot weather body temperature does not change. After a spinal cord injury your body temperature may rise on hot days or drop on cold ones. You may also be at risk for a serious condition called autonomic dysreflexia. This can occur when something has happened to the body below the level of injury and you cannot feel it. A message is sent through the nerves but it is blocked before reaching the brain. Because your nerves cannot effectively communicate the cause of the problem your blood pressure may rise. Common causes and symptoms of autonomic dysreflexia can be reviewed with the nursing staff. Sex and Intimacy Sex, sexuality, and intimacy are all closely related to each other. Feeling attractive and happy, being attracted to others, having and keeping relationships, physical intercourse, and being able to have children are all part sex and intimacy. After a spinal cord injury, there are often changes in these areas. For both men and women, losses in sensation may result in a need to find new ways to experience pleasure. Men may have changes in erectile function, ejaculations, and fertility. In women fertility is unchanged. Men and women should feel comfortable discussing issues related to sexual intimacy with their health care providers. Feelings and Reactions Not only is your body affected by a spinal cord injury, but also emotions are very much involved. It may help to know that most persons with a spinal cord injury go through several different emotional reactions including feeling down, depressed and angry. You may ask, "Why me?" Sometimes you will not feel like doing anything at all. For some people the worst part is not being able to do everything for themselves. It can be very upsetting when you must rely on others to do things for you. Most people say it helps to talk about feelings. If you talk to others about your feelings it is easier for them to help you; otherwise, it is hard for people to know what you are going through. You may find it helpful to talk to someone who has experienced a spinal cord injury. The Shirley Ryan AbilityLab of Chicago has a Peer Visitor program and can arrange for a visit from someone who has had a similar injury that you can talk to. Talk to your care manager or therapist to set this up. Shirley Ryan AbiltyLab provides ways to adapt and learn the new ABILITY each person has. Although the techniques and ways of doing things may be different than pre injury, SRALab provides you with adaptations and new ways of going about daily life. The Information Sheet "The Nervous System" will give you a general idea of what damage to the spinal cord does by specific levels. It is important to know that the level of damage, and whether the injury is complete or incomplete, make a difference. Also, other important factors such as general health, age, fitness, size and motivation, determine how much you can do for yourself. This content is for informational purposes only. It does not replace the advice of a physician or other health care professional. Reliance on this site's content is solely at your own risk. Shirley Ryan AbilityLab disclaims any liability for injury or damages resulting from the use of any site content. © Shirley Ryan AbilityLab (formerly Rehabilitation Institute of Chicago) Henry B. Betts LIFE Center – (312) 238-5433 – https://www.sralab.org/lifecenter

Symptoms of pressure ulcers

Pressure ulcers can affect any part of the body that's put under pressure. They're most common on bony parts of the body, such as the heels, elbows, hips and base of the spine.

They often develop gradually, but can sometimes form in a few hours.

Early symptoms

Early symptoms of a pressure ulcer include:

- part of the skin becoming discoloured – people with pale skin tend to get red patches, while people with dark skin tend to get purple or blue patches

- discoloured patches not turning white when pressed

- a patch of skin that feels warm, spongy or hard

- pain or itchiness in the affected area

Later symptoms

The skin may not be broken at first, but if the pressure ulcer gets worse, it can form:

- an open wound or blister – a category two pressure ulcer
- a deep wound that reaches the deeper layers of the skin – a category three pressure ulcer
- a very deep wound that may reach the muscle and bone – a category four pressure ulcer

- red, swollen skin
- pus coming from the pressure ulcer or wound
- cold skin and a fast heartbeat.
- severe or worsening pain
- a high temperature (fever) of 38C (100.4F) or above

These symptoms could be a sign of a serious infection that needs to be treated as soon as possible.

Spinal Cord Injury: Autonomic Dysreflexia

Topic Overview

Autonomic dysreflexia is a syndrome in which there is a sudden onset of excessively high blood pressure. It is more common in people with spinal cord injuries that involve the thoracic nerves of the spine or above (T6 or above).
Be prepared to call your spinal cord injury therapist, **911**, or other emergency services if you or the person with the spinal cord injury (SCI) has the symptoms of autonomic dysreflexia. If you or a caregiver cannot treat it promptly and correctly, it may lead to seizures, stroke, and even death.
Symptoms include:
- A pounding headache.
- A flushed face and/or red blotches on the skin above the level of spinal injury.
- Sweating above the level of spinal injury.
- Nasal stuffiness.
- Nausea.
- A slow heart rate (bradycardia).
- Goose bumps below the level of spinal injury.
- Cold, clammy skin below the level of spinal injury.
  If you feel you have autonomic dysreflexia:
- Sit up straight, or raise your head so you are looking straight ahead. If you can lower your legs,

do so. You need to be sitting upright until your blood pressure is back to normal.
- Loosen or take off any tight clothing or accessories. This includes braces, <u>catheter</u> tape, socks or stockings, shoes, and bandages.
- Empty your bladder by draining your Foley catheter or using your catheter.
- Use digital stimulation to empty your bowel.
- Check your skin for red spots that mean you might have a pressure injury.
- If possible, check your blood pressure every 5 minutes to see if it improves.
- Call your doctor, even if symptoms go away and your blood pressure is decreasing.
- If the symptoms return, repeat the above steps and go to the emergency room or call emergency services.

Autonomic dysreflexia occurs when something happens to your body below the level of your injury. This can be a pain or irritant (such as tight clothing or something pinching your skin) or a normal function that your body may not notice (such as having a full bladder and needing to urinate). These situations trigger an automatic reaction that causes your blood pressure to go up. As your blood pressure goes up, your heartbeat slows and may become irregular. Your body cannot restore your blood pressure to normal because of your spinal cord damage. The only way to return things to normal is to change the situation—for example, by removing tight clothing or emptying your bladder.

The following are some frequent causes of autonomic dysreflexia and how you can prevent them.

How to prevent autonomic dysreflexia

Cause	Prevention
Overfull bladder Urinary tract infections (UTIs)	Follow your bladder management program.
Overfull bowel or constipation Gastrointestinal problems such as gallstones, stomach ulcers, or gastritis	Follow your bowel management program. Eat fibre and consume fluids as your doctor suggests.

<u>Pressure injuries</u> <u>Ingrown nails</u> Other skin problems	Check your skin daily. Make sure all clothing or devices fit correctly.
Sexual activity	Be aware that sexual activity can cause the condition. Discuss this with your doctor.
Broken bones or other injuries Tight clothing or devices Extreme temperatures or quick temperature changes	Be aware that these can cause the condition. Discuss this with your doctor. Make sure all clothing and devices fit correctly.

https://www.healthlinkbc.ca/health-topics/ug2980

What is autonomic dysreflexia?

Autonomic dysreflexia (AD) is a potentially life-threatening medical emergency that affects people with spinal cord injuries at the T6 level or higher. Although rare, some people with T7 and T8 injuries can develop AD. For most people, AD can be easily treated as well as prevented. The key is knowing your baseline blood pressure, triggers, and symptoms.

When triggered, AD requires quick and correct action or there may be serious consequence such as a stroke. Because many health professionals are not familiar with this condition, it is important for people who are at risk for AD, including the people close to them, to recognize the symptoms and know how to act.

It's important for at-risk individuals to know their baseline blood pressure values and to communicate to healthcare providers how to identify as well as manage an AD emergency.

Some of the signs of AD include high blood pressure, pounding headache, flushed face, sweating above the level of injury, goose flesh below the level of injury, nasal stuffiness, nausea, and a slow pulse (slower than 60 beats per minute). Symptoms will vary based on the individual.

Causes of AD

Autonomic dysreflexia is caused by an irritant below the level of injury, including:

- Bladder: irritation of the bladder wall, urinary tract infection, blocked catheter or overfilled collection bag.
- Bowel: distended or irritated bowel, constipation or impaction, haemorrhoids or anal infections.
- Other causes include skin infection or irritation, cuts, bruises, abrasions or pressure sores (decubitus ulcers), ingrown toenails, burns (including sunburn and burns from hot water) and tight or restrictive clothing.
AD can also be triggered by sexual activity, menstrual cramps, labour and delivery, ovarian cysts, abdominal conditions (gastric ulcer, colitis, peritonitis) or bone fractures.

What to do when AD is triggered

If AD is suspected, the first thing to do is sit up or raise the head to 90 degrees. If you can lower your legs, do so. Next, loosen or remove any constricting clothing, and be sure to check your blood pressure every five minutes.

An individual with SCI above T6 often has a normal systolic blood pressure in the 90-110 mm Hg range.

- A blood pressure reading of 20mm to 40mm Hg above baseline in adults may be a sign of autonomic dysreflexia.

- 15mm above baseline in children, and 15mm to 20mm above baseline in adolescents may be a sign of autonomic dysreflexia.
  Most importantly, locate and remove the offending stimulus, if possible. Begin by looking for your most common causes: bladder, bowel, tight clothing, skin issues. Keep in mind as you remove the cause that your AD may get worse before it gets better.

What happens during an episode of AD?

Autonomic dysreflexia indicates over-activity of the autonomic nervous system – the part of the system that controls things you don't have to think about, such as heart rate, breathing and digestion.

A noxious stimulus (would be painful if one could sense it) below the injury level sends nerve impulses to the spinal cord; they travel upward until blocked at the level of injury.

Since these impulses cannot reach the brain, the body doesn't respond as it would normally. A reflex is activated that increases activity of the sympathetic portion of the autonomic nervous system. This results in a narrowing of the blood vessels, which causes a rise in blood pressure.

Nerve receptors in the heart and blood vessels detect this rise in blood pressure and send a message to the brain. The brain then sends a message to the heart, causing the heartbeat to slow down and the blood vessels above the level of injury to dilate. However, since the brain is not able to send messages below the level of injury, blood pressure cannot be regulated. The body is confused and can't sort out the situation.

Generally speaking, medications are used only if the offending stimulus cannot be identified and removed, or when an episode of AD persists even after the suspected cause has been removed.

A potentially useful agent is nitro glycerine paste (applied topically above level of injury). Nifedipine and nitrates are commonly used, in immediate-release form. Hydralazine, mecamylamine, diazoxide, and phenoxybenzamine might also be used.

If an erectile dysfunction drug (e.g., Cialis, Viagra) has been used within 24-hours, other medications should be considered as blood pressure could drop dangerously low.

For the most part, autonomic dysreflexia can be prevented. Keep catheters clean and adhere to your catheterization and bowel schedules.

https://www.christopherreeve.org/living-with-paralysis/health/secondary-conditions/autonomic-dysreflexia

Printed in Great Britain
by Amazon